CW01457565

THE GLOBAL CASINO

THE GLOBAL CASINO

How Wall Street Gambles with People
and the Planet

Ann Pettifor

V

VERSO

London • New York

First published by Verso 2026

The manufacturer's authorized representative in the EU for product safety (GPSR)
is LOGOS EUROPE, 9 rue Nicolas Poussin, 17000, La Rochelle, France
contact@logoseurope.eu

1 3 5 7 9 10 8 6 4 2

Verso
UK: 6 Meard Street, London W1F 0EG
US: 207 East 32nd Street, New York, NY 10016
versobooks.com

Verso is the imprint of New Left Books

ISBN-13: 978-1-80429-722-3
ISBN-13: 978-1-80429-724-7 (UK EBK)
ISBN-13: 978-1-80429-725-4 (US EBK)

British Library Cataloguing in Publication Data
A catalogue record for this book is available from the British Library

Library of Congress Cataloging-in-Publication Data
A catalog record for this book is available from the Library of Congress

Typeset in Garamond by Biblichor.co.uk
Printed and bound by CPI Group (UK) Ltd, Croydon CR0 4YY

Dedicated to the memory of the international political economist Susan Strange, author of Casino Capitalism *(1986)*

Financial markets were dominated by insane gambling to get in at the bottom, just as they were dominated in the boom by insane gambling to get out at the top . . . It is truly remarkable, that the paper value of all the railways and public utilities, after having fallen to one tenth of what it had been two years previously, has then proceeded to double itself within five weeks.

For this is no more than a vivid illustration of the disadvantages of running a country's development and enterprise as a by-product of a casino.

John Maynard Keynes, *The General Theory of Employment, Interest and Money* (1936)

My concern is . . . the consequences for ordinary people who have never been asked if they wanted to gamble their jobs, their savings, their income in this casino form of capitalism.

Susan Strange, *Mad Money* (1998)

Contents

Introduction

The hardest thing of all to see is what is really there.

J. A. Baker, *The Peregrine*

This book is about the insane gambling of international financial markets and the direct impact of their activities on our pensions, daily bread, energy, and housing; but also on the biosphere. Global financial markets and their gambling habits are largely invisible to non-economists and the wider public. Echoing both Keynes and the brilliant international political economist Susan Strange – to whom this book is dedicated – I have characterised today's system of financial market speculation as a 'Global Casino'.

The book was at its final editing stage when the Trump Shock of 2 April 2025 disrupted globalisation, the economic system that since the 1960s has powered today's financial markets. The Shock initially caused chaos in the Global Casino and threatened the liberal world order led by Western governments and dominated by the United States and its hegemonic world reserve currency, the US dollar. In the real world it intensified competition between the United States and China and triggered debates about the likely collapse of the world trading system and therefore the international world order we call globalisation. The Shock followed a post-COVID reality which had made the public increasingly aware of climate change and of the likelihood and impact of natural disasters. Above all, the Trump Shock empowered the far right across the world and increasingly dominated the social and political agenda.

The striking thing about the debates that followed Donald Trump's election to a second presidential term is that most ignored the role of the international financial system and open capital markets in both causing and amplifying global imbalances in trade and financial flows. Commentators tended to ignore the financial system's role in compounding both private and public debt levels. They ignored both the divisive and disruptive role played by the financial system in generating inequality, both within and between nations, and the system's role in amplifying the extraction of nature's finite resources. Instead, commentary was largely confined to the role of the trading system in triggering imbalances, the demand for tariffs, and the part played by multilateral institutions like the WTO, the IMF and the World Bank. There was scarcely any debate about an out-of-control financial system that I believe to be at the heart of public disillusionment with globalisation – a system that must be managed if we are to repair social contracts, recover trust in our democratic system, trade fairly with each other and address the threat of biosphere collapse.

At the heart of the globalised financial system is the United States' currency, the US dollar, which acts as the world's reserve currency – a globally recognised currency used in international trade and global finance. About 80 per cent of all cross-border trade (outside Europe) is invoiced in US dollars. At least 40 per cent of the paper US dollars in circulation by value, worth more than $1 trillion, are held outside the United States.[1] Most of the world's central banks deposit in good faith the wealth and international investments of their country – their foreign exchange reserves – in US dollars, and in the central banks of the US, UK and EU.

Before the Trump Shock, China and members of the G20 group of countries were made uneasy by the way in which international sovereignty immunity rights were violated by rich countries, with the confiscation of the foreign reserves of countries like Afghanistan and Russia. The BRICS countries (Brazil, Russia, India, China and South Africa) recognised that the United States could as easily confiscate *their* central bank reserves, and so at G20 annual meetings they began discussing alternatives to the US dollar as the world's reserve currency.

Then in 2025, as a result of the Trump Shock and in particular his 'Liberation Day' announcement of high tariffs on US imports, the US dollar began to weaken. By May 2025 it was 10 per cent below what its value should have been relative to other currencies, given interest rate differentials between the US and other countries. That had never happened before. Whenever US interest rates rose, the US dollar strengthened, and capital was flushed out of the markets of so-called emerging markets – countries like Brazil, Russia, India, China and South Africa – and was funnelled into US financial markets. The effect was always to strengthen the US dollar and crush the value of currencies around the world – especially those of low-income countries.

The weakening of the US dollar in 2025 was an unprecedented reversal of this process.

Britain's former prime minister Gordon Brown quickly entered the debate with a call for 'how we should proceed'. He used his undoubted authority to assert that 'globalisation is now rejected by millions as a "free for all" that has not been fair to all'. He called for a 'Roosevelt-inspired declaration of international cooperation' to promote a set of 'principles and basic freedoms – against the use of force and protectionism, and for the self-determination of nations and national social contracts that would bridge the divide between rich and poor'.[2]

Given that a large part of the purpose behind financial globalisation was to remove the power of self-determination from governments and to weaken the adoption of policies 'that would bridge the divide between rich and poor', this must be a call for managing the Global Casino.

Yet Gordon Brown's reasoning (as expressed in his article) omits globalised money and finance. (He is not alone in that. Most orthodox economists construct models of the economy that 'cannot find room for money'.[3]) The assumption is that both economies and corporations are managed, regulated and taxed by the world's parliaments, state treasuries and central banks. That approach leads societies to blame and punish governments at elections for economic failure. The truth is more complicated: governments are often not to blame. Indeed, many governments, especially in the south, are victims of an opaque, but powerful, private system of largely unregulated markets that oblige governments to orient away from the interests of the domestic economy and to compete globally for private finance, investment and markets. A competitive system that in its current form will quickly suffocate Brown's correct call for the urgent need for international cooperation and coordination to stabilise the world economic order.

The conventional view of the relationship between the economy and democracy is thus a delusion, just as the conventional view that the climate was the same as the weather was once a widely held delusion. We, and the economies we inhabit, are not governed by elected politicians and their public servants. Instead, the value of the economy and of a nation's currency and its interest rates, as well as the levels of investment that ought to provide livelihoods and both economic and ecological security, are all economic levers largely wielded by unaccountable and irresponsible financiers operating in the international financial system. Together with technocrats at central banks, the decision-making and activities of global bankers, asset managers, hedge fund owners and private equity professionals – who never stand for election. They affect our economies, daily lives and livelihoods in powerful ways.

For many, including most mainstream economists, the focus on the economy is narrow and earthbound, set at what is called the *micro* level: the individual, the household and the firm. Microeconomists tend to overlook the impact of the international system and to focus on events in the everyday economy, which happens to be the title of a book by British Chancellor of the Exchequer Rachel Reeves.[4] Ms Reeves's book defines 'three constituent parts of this political economy: work and wages, families and households, and the local places people belong to'.

The domestic focus is based on the assumptions of conventional microeconomics. Namely, that the demand for and supply of capital, goods and services depend on a multitude of rational decision makers in competitive markets.

I hope to empower readers to view, understand and then challenge that narrow view and to embrace the global *macroeconomic* system and its role in determining national levels of investment, employment and output. Just as we have learned to make the distinction between the weather and the climate, between what is local and what is planetary, so we must learn about a financialised system that operates beyond our daily experience of the economy, even while it impacts our daily lives – often detrimentally.

Such an approach is vital not just for economic reasons, but also democratic ones. Contrary to our understanding of democratic political power, the financial system's clout eclipses the authority of even the world's powerful elected governments. There is no clearer evidence of finance's power than billionaire donations to pro-Trump political action committees (as well as those of presidential hopeful, Kamala Harris) and the capture of the US Congress by Wall Street.

America is not alone. The private financial system has corrupted and bribed politicians across the world, including ex-president Jacob Zuma of South Africa, who created the blueprint for what South Africans called 'state capture' – systemic political corruption in which private interests significantly influence a state's decision-making process to their own advantage.

Democratic institutions have everywhere been hollowed out and defanged by those active in the top ranks of the financial system. Consequently, under the current world order, we are effectively governed by wealthy and powerful players in markets based in Silicon Valley, Wall Street, the Chicago Mercantile Exchange and the City of London. (From now on I will bracket all these players under the term *Wall Street*.) President Roosevelt was explicit about these enemies of democracy. In a famous speech in Madison Square Garden in 1936, he explained that his administration had to 'struggle with the old enemies of peace – business and financial monopoly, speculation, reckless banking, class antagonism, sectionalism, war profiteering.

'They had begun to consider the Government of the United States as a mere appendage to their own affairs. We now know that Government by organized money is just as dangerous as Government by organized mob.'5

Government by organised money has become unbearable for human society. Financial markets that dictate high prices of unaffordable services essential to humanity – services like water, housing, energy, health and education – have triggered powerful political reactions. Society has turned to strongmen, dictators and authoritarians for 'protection' from markets. The reasoning, as Karl Polanyi explained in 1944, is straightforward: government by markets could not exist for long before 'annihilating the human and natural substance of society; it would have physically destroyed man [*sic*] and transformed his surroundings into a wilderness'.[6]

Inevitably, society took measures to protect itself, he continued. But whatever measures it took – for example, the election of Donald Trump, who promised protection from Chinese and Mexican markets – impaired those markets, disorganised industrial life and endangered society in other ways.

If society is to restore stability to the economic system, to manage climate breakdown and the power of the fossil interest, then we must first transform, regulate and manage the Global Casino. Only then can we hope to build a fairer and more stable world order.

What Is the Global Casino?

To understand the system, it might help to shine a light on the activities of those operating in the Casino, a financial 'territory' where few if any laws and regulations restrain speculation and gambling. The Casino supersedes states and permits capital – unlike labour and goods – to move across borders without encountering meaningful barriers or friction. One individual illuminates the system's workings more than any other and alerts us to the dangers of what Susan Strange called 'mad money'.[7] He is the Korean billionaire Masayoshi Son, and his Japanese company is known as SoftBank.

Back in December 2016, Masayoshi Son was being driven through New York to a meeting with the newly elected President Trump.[8] Son was nervous and excited. Steve Schwarzman, the private-equity billionaire boss of Blackstone and a Trump backer, had helped prep him for this first-ever meeting with the New York real estate developer. The advice was to play to Trump's vanity. Drawing on other people's money, Son adjusted, simplified and inflated SoftBank's offer to the new president: 50,000 American jobs with a $15 billion investment from his company.

Sitting beside him in the car as they sped to the meeting was a young, relaxed Israeli with long black hair. Son had invited him to make a sales pitch. The young man's grand vision was for a new world of work: 'cool high-tech office space with cushions, Pelotons and plenty of free booze'.[9] Within minutes of listening to this proposition, Son pulled out his iPad, waved his hands around and sketched the outlines of a $4.4 billion napkin contract to invest in 'an office-space-leasing company which promised to conquer the world'.

As Damon Runyon, who wrote about New York gamblers in *Guys and Dolls*, might have said, $4.4 billion is a lot of potatoes. Son's young messiah was Adam Neumann. The company's name was WeWork. Son's valuation and investment caused WeWork's projected value to rocket as it began to expand. 'Masa's multi-billion-dollar pledge to WeWork fitted a pattern of seemingly irrational decisions to invest mind-blowing amounts of money on founders he'd barely spoken to', writes his biographer.[10]

Some years later, and in an even grander fit of delusion, Neumann calculated that WeWork's revenue would rise exponentially to $101 billion. Neumann promised Son that by 2023 the company would have acquired 1 billion square feet of office space, twice the size of the whole Manhattan real estate market. In return for this vision, he demanded a $70 billion investment from SoftBank's Vision Fund.

Masayoshi Son had not learned a thing. The gambling bug struck again. He obliged Neumann. He went further. He 'rolled out the red carpet', writes Lionel Barber, and 'magicked up a WeWork valuation on his iPad . . . in yellow ink he scribbled $10 T [trillion] and underlined it twice. At the time the value of the entire US stock market was $30 trillion.'[11]

Those crazy valuations and Son's speculative investment did not sit well with his fellow investors. On Christmas Eve 2018, while Adam Neumann was surfing in Hawaii, readying for the deal to close, his iPhone rang. It was Masayoshi Son. The deal, he said, was dead. In November 2023, WeWork, whose office-leasing business model was crushed by the COVID lockdown, filed for Chapter 11 bankruptcy.

The world Masayoshi Son and Adam Neumann occupy is the Global Casino. Son, whose Korean-Japanese father ran pachinko (arcade game) gambling parlours, rose heroically to riches from the poverty of his childhood. Thanks to financial globalisation, by 2000, he had ridden the dot-com bubble and was briefly the richest man in the world, according to his biography, *Gambling Man: The Wild Ride of Japan's Masayoshi Son*.[12] When the dot-com bubble burst, Son lost 97 per cent of his fortune, around $70 billion. Like any gambling addict, that loss did not deter him.

Unlike Steve Jobs or Bill Gates or even Elon Musk, Masayoshi Son is no tech innovator. Instead, he was and is the single largest foreign speculator in capitalist America and communist China: the biggest start-up funder in the world, and the boss of one of the top-ten most indebted firms, continually threatening a financial implosion. In the teeth of the global credit crunch of 2008, SoftBank's vast borrowing and its off-piste adventures in subprime derivatives came back to haunt it. Once again, Son was forced into a fire sale of his personal shareholding to meet margin calls at that time. 'I lost almost all my worldly assets,' he confessed to Barber in 2008.[13] He did not take long to recover.

Not everyone recovered from the global financial crisis so quickly. Millions lost jobs and the roof over their heads. Others became heavily indebted, while firms were bankrupted or restructured. The anxiety and anguish caused by these losses and changes are intense: marriages break up, suicides occur and individuals become depressed, lose their sense of dignity and suffer mental breakdowns. Government debt rises as an inevitable consequence of economic failure, and so does private debt. Public services are slashed, and the weak and vulnerable are made victims of a crisis they did not help cause and for which they cannot be blamed.

Like other gamblers in the Global Casino, Masayoshi Son continues to operate and profit from an international financial system that is largely deregulated and that facilitates the movement of speculative capital across the world's borders without oversight or hindrance. Thanks to public subsidies and the backing of other people's money, Masayoshi Son is back to gambling. In December 2024, he flew to Washington for another meeting with the newly re-elected President Trump and announced a multibillion-dollar investment in AI, doubling the similar promise he had made to Trump in his first term, a promise that *Forbes* magazine argued had 'mixed results'.[14] *Forbes* also reported that in the week of 6 April 2025, Masayoshi Son's net worth dropped by $2.1 billion to $23.6 billion amid the mayhem that surrounded President Trump's radical tariffs announcement.

Globalisation

> Increased rates of problem gambling and gambling harms have shown to be linked to the policies of governments. Despite evidence of correlation between availability and harm, many jurisdictions have increased both the availability and promotion of gambling. Almost all jurisdictions have some sort of interest in or dependency on the profit from gambling.[15]

This quote, from an academic study of domestic gambling policies, is just as applicable to the policies of governments that have enabled gambling at the global level.

The modern world of financial globalisation was constructed in the years that followed the 1971 collapse of the post-war Bretton Woods system of managed financial and trade flows. First slowly and then rapidly (after the 'Volcker shock' in 1980, which saw US interest rates rise to 20 per cent), government policies changed. Barriers to the movement of trade and capital were broken down and 'free trade' became the mantra. The globalised and financialised system that is today's Global Casino was born.

We are all familiar with globalisation. It has deep roots in British economic liberalism and nineteenth-century imperialism. The theoretical foundations of the system were laid in the late eighteenth century by Adam Smith and David Hume. They used a liberal idea imported from Spain and France, where liberal ideas had no connection to free market theory, to describe their favoured pre-political free market system.[16] In contrast to the Europeans, the British version of liberalism – 'Pax Britannica' – fused (however disingenuously) the political ideas of rule of law and civil liberties with the economic maxims of free trade and free markets.

This unique and ultimately revolutionary combination of political and economic ideas was driven first by nineteenth-century innovations in British monetary policy that aided investment abroad, and second by sterling's role as the world's reserve currency. The growing prestige of the Bank of England, the military power of the state, the dynamism of the City of London and access to cheap (and dirty) energy helped power, protect and finance Britain's nineteenth-century exporters.

These conditions prepared the ground for the emergence of Britain's colonial empire and its great imperialists, embodied by Cecil John Rhodes. To protect his South African wealth, Rhodes engaged the British state in the futile and costly Second Boer War. J. A. Hobson, an economist whose reputation is tainted by anti-Semitism, was the *Guardian*'s correspondent during the Boer War. From that perspective he analysed Britain's liberal nineteenth-century global trading and financial system in his 1902 book, *Imperialism*.

Britain's wealthy, Hobson argued, bolstered by the power of unregulated capital mobility, export subsidies and tax breaks, preferred to invest their surplus wealth abroad, rather than investing in the home economy. The nation's wealthy favoured markets in countries like South Africa or Argentina, where capital was scarce, wages were low and land cheap. That led to increased production at lower costs. However, because of low investment and low incomes both at home and in the colonies, citizens did not have the purchasing power to consume all that was produced. Aided by the mobility of cross-border capital flows, investors then searched for even more foreign markets where returns were high.

With time the nineteenth-century version of globalisation took hold.

As more and more of Britain's wealth was channelled abroad, the toxic combination of inequality at home and imperialism abroad raised political tensions, much as they do today. Only twelve years after Hobson's *Imperialism* was published, Britain and the world were plunged into a catastrophic world war.

Today in Trump's America, Apple's Tim Cook, Tesla's Elon Musk and Nvidia's Jensen Huang have profited immensely from globalisation. While their businesses differ, like their predecessors, modern plutocrats prefer to channel investment and production into low-wage countries like China, Vietnam and India and to direct their profits into low-tax domains like Ireland.

China's counterparts to the power of American billionaires are the bosses of the heavily subsidised and state-backed corporations that churn out goods channelled into markets in North America, Europe and Africa. Wealth in China is also highly concentrated. The top 10 per cent of the population hold approximately 67 per cent of China's wealth.[17] The top .001 per cent own 5.8 per cent of China's total wealth, roughly equivalent to that of the bottom 50 per cent. The share of China's national income earned by the top 10 per cent of the population increased from 27 per cent in 1978 to 41 per cent in 2015, while the share earned by the bottom 50 per cent (a group that includes 536 million adults) dropped from 27 to 15 per cent. But unlike the West, investment rates have remained staggeringly high.

Trade wars, argue the economists Klein and Pettis, originate with inequality at home: in conflicts between wealthy, subsidised, low-taxed exporters of capital – the 1 per cent – and the majority of people within a country, who endure insecurity, falling or stagnant real incomes and rising levels of taxation.[18]

In 1971, the year President Nixon dismantled the Bretton Woods rules-based order that had delivered a golden age in economics, US workers shared 51 per cent of the nation's annual income (GDP). By 2023 that share had fallen by almost 10 per cent to 42.6 per cent of the GDP.

America's richest 1 per cent of households averaged 139 times as much income as the bottom 20 per cent in 2021, according to the US Congressional Budget Office. Over the past three decades, America's most affluent families have added to their net worth, while those on the bottom have dipped into 'negative wealth', as their debts exceed the value of their assets. During the COVID-19 pandemic, the combined wealth of all US billionaires increased by $2.071 trillion (70.3 per cent) between 18 March 2020 and 15 October 2021, from approximately $2.947 trillion to $5.019 trillion. Of the more than 700 US billionaires, the richest five (Jeff Bezos, Bill Gates, Mark Zuckerberg, Larry Page and Elon Musk) saw a 123 per cent increase in their combined wealth.

In the United States (as elsewhere) those tensions were exploited by the Trump campaign, which blamed inequality and falling living standards on migrants and foreigners – Mexicans, Chinese and even Canadians – not on Trump's tax-avoiding, Silicon Valley–based billionaire backers. America's class wars echo the domestic and international tensions that led to the collapse of nineteenth-century financial globalisation. It is unclear whether today's politicians are aware of the parallels.

What is financialised globalisation?

Today, 6 billion (75 per cent) of the world's people have bank accounts, an expansion that occurred alongside the breakdown of international barriers to the movement of money across borders.[19] The permissiveness of the globalised system has driven a spectacular rise in international shopping, trade and tourism. That is how many people view globalisation, through the shiny lenses of the internet: social media, the Amazon website, YouTube and other glossy Silicon Valley platforms.

But there is much more going on – and it is not pretty. Unlike most goods, services and commodities that traverse the global trading system, financial globalisation is a process that transforms almost everything owned or traded into mobile, tradeable financial assets. Financial assets, unlike commodities (copper, soybeans and oil) are intangible, riddled with complexity and invisible to most of humanity. They are paper copies of real assets – commodities – and are used to bet on the movement of prices up or down. They're like bets on the horses by those who don't own horses. But unlike horse race betting, they are incredibly dangerous.

To grasp why, we need to understand that financialised assets are based on something ephemeral, a social construct: money. And all money is credit – an obligation, a 'promise to pay': a series of human obligations and claims on both present and future human and ecological resources.

Credit money in turn is based on trust, upheld by regulation and law. The grave danger posed by the globalised financial system is that it is largely lawless and unregulated. Lawlessness undermines trust – the very thing that gives money obligations value.

Yet it is lawlessness that has led to the financialisation of care homes, transport systems, food delivery systems and even mobile phones. It has transformed those services into 'rentable' financial assets for their owners. These assets, like the income from a property, generate rising levels of 'rent', or returns, over fixed periods of time. They are no longer just public services, designed to deliver care, health or food. Instead, they have been transformed into financial assets whose value for the owner consists above all in contracts that are confidently expected to generate streams of income into an unknown future. In the financial 'stratosphere', paper financial assets can be used as gambling chips.

Thanks to the deregulation of globalisation, the rent or income from financial assets like transport, care homes or food delivery services (think Uber and DoorDash) can be swept up into the financial system and delivered to an owner based in, say, faraway Silicon Valley. The cross-border movement of that proverbial rent into the bank accounts of Uber and DoorDash can be achieved at the click of an app button and without any customs checks at borders. In that sense, the profits and capital gains made from financialised assets are very different from profits made from the global investment and trade in commodities. Unlike finance, trade confronts friction at almost every border in the form of tariffs, standards and regulations of one kind or another.

The danger posed by the globalised financial system is that it operates beyond the reach of regulatory democracy and the law. As such it undermines society's most important values: honesty, integrity, accountability and trust. The corruption of those values ultimately undermines trust in politicians and, with it, democracy.

Understanding the Ephemeral Thing That Is Money

Money, unlike commodities, land and goods, is not a thing (as explained above). It is not gold, or land or a seashell, nor is it a crypto coin. Money is inherently a *social relationship*, a social convention built on trust, upheld by regulation and contracts and enforced by law.

Crypto coins are based on lawlessness and therefore cannot function as money. Crypto currencies are in effect Ponzi schemes: 'an old-fashioned fraud wrapped in modern technology', writes Erica Stanford.[20] A fraud that deploys scams, hacks, pump and dump schemes and money laundering for dubious and often criminal purposes. So while crypto coins are assets that can be bartered, traded and speculated on, they cannot act as a currency and cannot ever be used as money. To become money, the crypto community would have to regulate to uphold and enforce that social quality vital to the nature of the obligations we call money: trust.

Gold, paper notes, coins and debit and credit cards are all tangible representations of the quantity of obligations – money – and the quality of trust held by any one individual. A Dubai First Royale Mastercard, for example, has no positive balances in the account, but suggests a high degree of trust in the wealth, and ability to pay, of its owner. Those with lower incomes are given more modest credit cards. While credit cards have no savings or deposits in the account (in fact deposits are forbidden by credit card issuers who make money from the credit, and not deposits), the card represents the credibility of the owner. The value of these cards lies in the degree to which they are trusted.

Once promises circulate and proliferate, the monetary system becomes ever more complex. At all times and in all circumstances, trust is fundamental to the system, and to any monetary relationship or institution like a bank or central bank. If society is to make advances (credit) and agree to settlements (debt), then in any arrangements for money (credit, debt) there must be trust, cooperation and responsibility – and, because of human frailty, these arrangements must be enforced by laws and regulations.

The Global Casino has no such arrangements, laws or regulations, even while it is tethered to the real institutions of credit, laws and regulations and is periodically bailed out by the regulated economy. Like the disguised wolf in the fairy tale, the mask of complexity and invisibility ensures that today's financialised capitalism is beyond the reach of the law, regulators and elected politicians. Its protagonists, such as Masayoshi Son, are largely unknown, and its transactions immaterial.

The system's design, I contend, is intentional. By operating beyond the reach of any nation's laws and regulations, financiers have opportunities to avoid taxation and to exploit and extract wealth from people and the planet – the real world to which they are also tethered.

John Maynard Keynes deplored the deregulated system of rentier capitalism that so disrupted the global economy of the 1920s and '30s and inflicted two catastrophic world wars on humanity. Susan Strange was determined that the Global Casino should no longer remain hidden from public view and used her many publications to shine a light on the system. As far back as 1986 she dubbed the volatile, corrupt complex 'Casino Capitalism'.[21] Regrettably her analyses were largely ignored, even while she is held in high esteem by her largely academic admirers in the field of international political economy.[22]

The Global Casino

I have two reasons for choosing and reinforcing Susan Strange's framing. First, defining the spatial aspect of an apparently remote, deregulated financial system will make it more comprehensible. Second, the activities that take place in the often out-of-control Casino amount to little more than reckless gambling. Strange explains that in financial markets 'you may place bets on the future by dealing forward and by buying or selling options and all sorts of other recondite financial inventions'. She describes 'big bankers and brokers' as croupiers in this global financial casino, 'peddlers of systems to the gullible'. She may have added that they are also predators, exploiters and subordinators of most low-income countries.

Today, speculators within the Casino play with much larger stakes than those that were deployed in 1986 – trillions of US dollars. In the latest estimate from the Financial Stability Board, today's croupiers gamble in the world of *shadow banking* – a term used to describe bank-like activities that take place beyond the regulatory boundaries of states. Shadow banks hold financial assets valued at $217 trillion. These financial assets include the world's pensions, surpluses and other savings.[23] As explained previously, financial assets are different from physical assets in that they are liquid and intangible contracts, with only the stated, expected value found on a piece of paper. They represent claims (rent) on (expected) future income from assets like equities, bonds, pensions, mutual funds, insurance contracts, patents and intellectual property.

These financial assets are managed (and sometimes mismanaged) in the Global Casino by a range of largely unregulated companies. The Casino exercises far greater economic power today than when Strange warned us of its dangers in 1986. Instead of big bankers and brokers, today's croupiers are so-called Wall Street hedge funds (fund managers who seldom hedge but often gamble), asset management funds, private equity firms, sovereign wealth funds and pension funds, as well as individual financiers. Together they operate within the unregulated shadow banking system.

Those active in the Global Casino have the power to alter the daily existence of the world's people and its fragile ecosystem. Yet the system and its operators remain unaccountable, even when collectively they accelerate the extraction or destruction of nature's finite assets, cause a global financial meltdown, trigger a worldwide cost-of-living crisis or render millions of people homeless.

Widespread public ignorance of the Global Casino can easily be explained by the reluctance of mainstream economists to teach their students about money and the monetary system. As Claudio Borio of the Bank for International Settlements (the granddaddy of all central banks) complained in 2018: 'Money has been allowed to sink by the macroeconomics profession. And with little or no regrets.'[24] In other words, most macroeconomists neither teach, nor understand, nor think of money as important. Many consider money as simply a veil over real transactions in the economy, which is made up of the exchange of goods and services in production and consumption. As a result, ignorance of money and monetary systems is shared by politicians, journalists and commentators. Nor are domestic and international monetary systems subjects of popular debate, explanation and discussion. When crises occur, the spotlight seldom falls on the clandestine financial system, on those who exercise power within it and those who benefit richly from it.

This was well illustrated during the financial turbulence that followed the Trump 'Liberation Day' trade announcement of 2 April 2025, when the US president imposed an aggressive and bafflingly calculated set of tariffs on most of the world's economies. The announcement threatened to damage most economies and to disrupt the supposed rules-based system of international trade. It triggered volatility in the financial system and in markets for both stocks and US government bonds.

In the midst of the turmoil, hedge funds that had borrowed huge sums from shadow banks found that their collateral (government bonds) used to guarantee repayment of the borrowing were fast diminishing in value relative to the debts they owed. The fall in the value of those bonds (US Treasuries) was caused by an outflow of capital from the bond market as nervous owners of US Treasuries sold their bonds for cash. That outflow was in turn triggered by the president's reckless conduct, which undermined trust in the US government's ability to honour its obligations to repay debts (bonds) in full.

Forced by their creditors to sell bonds to raise cash to repay debts, hedge funds flooded the market with newly sold bonds.

Just as a farmer flooding a market with tomatoes would cause tomato prices to fall, this reaction caused bond prices to fall and yields on the bonds (the sum to be paid out when the bond expires) to rise. Thanks to the way in which the global system for managing interest rates have been marketised, higher yields (effectively interest on Treasury bills or bonds) would have impacted all borrowers in the wider economy and increased the cost of capital, for governments as well as for firms and households.

The disruption and the threat to the nation's financial stability caused Trump's Treasury secretary to pressure the president into a climbdown. The imposition of high tariffs was paused seven days later.

Few of Trump's supporters would have known about upheavals in bond markets. Many would have assumed the Democrats or politics forced the climbdown. Instead, it was heavily indebted bond market vigilantes active in the shadow banking sector who forced the change. That Trump got a bloody nose may be considered a good thing, but the incident reveals the power of the unaccountable financial system.

The Money System and the Fossil System

Actors in the privatised and globalised money system exercise immense power over the world's economies. Whereas in the past, interest rates and exchange rates were managed by central bankers, accountable to parliaments and governments, today market rates are set by actors in global financial markets. Finance ministers live in fear of markets that may disapprove of government spending plans. Private, speculative markets that, as punishment, will hike the prices (yields) on government bond sales while downgrading the value of a nation's currency by selling it in exchange for another.

This undemocratic system is the achievement of a few neo-liberal economists like Ludwig von Mises, F. A. Hayek and Lionel Robbins (among others), who, like Milton Friedman, regarded democracy as overrated and a 'potential threat to the functioning of the market order'.[25] Those economists used their professional status to defeat Keynesian policies for *public* (that is, democratic) authority over markets. Instead, they lobbied for the redesign and reform of states, laws and other institutions to ensure the establishment of private market authority over the economy. They sought to encase or protect markets (that is, investors, rentiers and speculators in those markets) from any intervention by sovereign, regulatory nation states and their elected representatives.[26] The globalisers, mostly based on Wall Street, had begun to achieve their goals by the early 1960s. Later they were helped in their mission by politicians like Presidents Nixon and Reagan and Prime Minister Thatcher.

Today, the deregulated money system largely ignores the threat of climate breakdown and finances the fossil system. The fossil system would quickly burn out were it not for the rocket fuel provided by Big Finance. Of the two, the financial system is the most consequential.

The two systems are different but share many qualities. In contrast to the financial system, the fossil system and its dirty emissions are tangible. They can be found, seen and touched anywhere in the world. Today, both systems are in full expansion mode. They continue to grow aggressively. However, both are volatile and unbalanced – and increasingly vulnerable to shocks and crises that quickly change their dynamics. Both are sources of global insecurity: climatic, environmental, social and economic. The free market policies that underpin the two systems have led to obscene levels of both financial and energy inequality and injustice, both within and between countries. And their largely deregulated financial and energy flows pass on risks to distant others – often from the rich north to the impoverished south.

Both the money and fossil systems are characterised by their masters' preference for the largely unregulated flow of assets and the build-up of stocks of said assets. In the case of finance, the flow is of credit. That is to say, easy money that builds up stocks of liabilities – debt. These debts are attached to individuals, corporations and governments and can periodically become unpayable and implode into global financial crises. Think of the credit crunch of 2008 that blew up the US mortgage market. In the case of fossils, the flow is of dirty energy that in time builds up stocks of carbon within the climate system. Carbon stocks are warming the planet and leading to the breakdown and weakening of nature's resilience.

These flows and stocks of money and fossil energy require the constant extraction and exploitation of nature's finite assets to maintain high rates of profit and capital gains and to repay debts. They are levels of extraction and exploitation that place humanity's life-support system at risk.[27] Their impacts include extreme weather events, deflation and inflation and recurring financial crises. In social terms they have led to the meltdown of trust in financial, political and scientific experts and democratic institutions. Most alarmingly, the largely unregulated actions of private actors and institutions in global markets have led to the increasingly rapid breakdown of the world's balanced life-support system: the climate and ecosystem.[28]

Who governs these two systems?

Power and governance over the two systems have, over time and with intention, been privatised. Governors of the money system are based in, and operate from, financial centres in Singapore,

Shanghai, Frankfurt, London and New York. After the 1960s, power was shifted away from elected politicians and central bank technocrats to private actors in global markets (often referred to in abstract terms as *market forces*, a phrase that renders both their power and actual governors invisible). Together with tame economists, weak regulators and compliant governments, Wall Street elites are architects of a system that by deliberate design is remote, invisible and unaccountable. That lack of accountability corrodes and corrupts democratic institutions. The lawlessness of the system encourages reckless speculation and irresponsibility.

Similarly, governors of the world's fossil markets are powerful traders and corporations, just as unseen and unaccountable. But energy prices are not solely determined by producers of fossil fuels. They are not fixed by the president of Russia, the king of Saudi Arabia, the prime minister of Norway, or the bosses of Shell, ExxonMobil and BP. Instead, prices of fossil fuels are determined by 'markets' – invisible traders, investors and speculators operating in detached global markets like the Chicago Mercantile Exchange.

This transfer of power away from the regulatory state, from democratic, public institutions, helps explain the impotence and inadequacy of today's politicians and policy-makers when faced with financial and energy imbalances. And that impotence – the failure and inability of elected politicians to use their power to regulate markets and address society's grievances – has led to public despair, to the rise of conspiracy theories and disinformation. Ultimately that hollowing out of democratic power has led to societal demands for protection from the arbitrary actions of markets and to the rise of far-right authoritarians – strongman politics – promising protection from globalised market forces.

Karl Polanyi blamed the collapse of nineteenth-century civilisation on the gold standard, the globalised financial system of its day. He regarded the ideas that lay behind the construction of the deregulated international gold standard as utopian. He believed that the continuation of the gold standard system would have physically destroyed societies and nature.[29] And so it proved in the 1930s and again today.

Our daily lives and livelihoods are increasingly disturbed and ruined by financial, political and ecological volatility, leading to periodic and sometimes catastrophic crises. Since the start of the twenty-first century, as awareness grew of the threat posed by ecological breakdown to human civilisation, societies have endured recurring crises. Over that same period, the global economy (and domestic economies) lurched from the Great Financial Crisis to the Global Financial Crisis (GFC) of 2007–9, from the 2009–10 European debt crisis to the 17 September 2019 collapse of the repo (shadow banking) market (which led to massive central bank bailouts). And from the February 2020 COVID-induced stock market and March 2020 shadow banking crash to the 2021–24 global cost-of-living crisis. All these crises have deregulated financial systems at their core.

Today, the global economy is once again in a state of grave disorder, thanks to the Trump administration's attack on the global trading system, and the threat of tariff wars. These financial and economic events strike from afar, like lightning or the winds of a super typhoon. Their impact results in both economic failure and ecosystem degradation. Public and private investment falls, jobs are lost, incomes are eroded. And all the while the owners of wealth make capital gains.

Governance of the globalised financial system, the world order, is discussed in passive terms. We are led to believe that global financial governance of the economies of the world is something that happens naturally, that there is an inherent stability in the system so no outside governance is needed.[30] And yet events continue to shock and disrupt the system, and no one can be found culpable. No one, it seems, was actually responsible for the Global Financial Crisis of 2007–9. Very few went to jail, and of those who did, most were from Iceland. Instead, the system was bailed out by the governors of the Federal Reserve of the United States and other central bankers.

And because mainstream economists had no explanation for the causes of the crisis and no proposals for reform, the system was not changed. Instead of stabilising it through radical reregulation, central bankers and policy-makers did the reverse: they began the step-by-step construction of a too-big-to-fail regime for Wall Street banks and other financial institutions. In the absence of any serious regulation, Wall Street players could not believe their luck. Before the GFC, banks on Wall Street and other financial centres faced the threat of bankruptcy – think Bear Stearns, Countrywide Financial or Northern Rock. Since the GFC, that threat has evaporated in large part because rich country OECD governments and their central banks have become bailout states.[31]

After the public sector bailouts of 2007–9, the Global Casino continued to behave as before, only this time private bankers and other financial institutions were confident they were too big to fail and too big to jail. Financiers continued to underwrite dangerously high levels of private and public debts in the shared expectation of future government bailouts. They lent much-needed capital (dollar loans) at usurious rates of interest to low-income countries, on the condition that taxpayers of rich governments effectively de-risk the loans and compensate private creditors if, and when, impoverished low-income countries should default.

Sure enough, in March 2020, a second global financial crisis occurred, this time triggered by a pandemic. Once again civil

servants at central banks quickly bailed out the system by expanding the money supply with more quantitative easing (QE) and
looser monetary policies (low, even negative interest rates),
while governments used fiscal policies to mitigate the damage to
businesses and households and to clear up the mess.

This was dramatically driven home on 18 May 2020 when
CBS News's Scott Pelley interviewed the governor of the Federal
Reserve, Jerome Powell. The Fed had just bailed out the Global
Casino in March 2020, as the pandemic was taking hold. Scott
Pelley asked the governor: 'Has the Fed done all it can do?'
Jerome Powell was emphatic: 'Well, there is a lot more we can do.
We're not out of ammunition by a long shot. No, there's, there's
really no limit to what we can do with these lending programs
that we have.'[32] Wall Street took note.

Central Banks were willing to do whatever it took to rectify
the risks and mistakes of the capitalist Global Casino, at the cost
of everyone else. And with not a moment's discussion of conditionality and reform.

Corruption and the Global Casino

Global markets in money, food and energy are an outgrowth of
an international financial system whose shaky foundation consists of freewheeling cross-border capital flows: unregulated
movements of capital and the largely unregulated creation of
credit or new money. These free-wheeling cross-border flows of
private capital escape the checks of regulators, customs officers
and tax collectors of democratic (and undemocratic) states, both
in the north and south. They are silent, invisible flows of money
that avoid and evade public, democratic authority. Unlike con-
tainer shipping or tourists visiting a foreign country, mobile
capital encounters almost no friction at the borders and custom

houses of the G7. Nor are they ever stopped and trapped in the Suez or Panama canals. They are unaffected by war and uprisings, as when Houthis in 2024 lobbed missiles at ships passing through the Gulf of Aden and diverted the flow of trade through the Southern Africa route.

One of the consequences of the global system of freewheeling cross-border flows of money is that it liberates and empowers corrupt politicians and officials, as well as terrorist organisations, mafias, fraudsters, thieves, money launderers and murderous drug cartels. But the most profound consequence of the global financial system is that its governors act effectively as an unelected and unaccountable world government. Susan Strange argued correctly in 1996 that

> both mafias and nation-states are under pressure from the forces of globalisation. For each to survive in the competition for shares of the world market, economic rationality means taking less account than in the past of kinship (or ethnicity) as the basis for a shared sense of community and the basis of legitimate authority. Yet for both this may be at the expense of social cohesion and the authority conferred by the sense of a common identity.[33]

These forces are especially effective in manipulating key economic levers to suit the narrow interests of 'wealth' among the world's billionaires and oligopolists, and against the interests of 'labour' – the majority who live by hand or brain. As noted above, the economic levers pulled include the rate of interest determined by a nation's central bank, the exchange rate of a nation's currency, the cross-border flow of capital for investment (loans and their price – the rate of interest). Finally, they have power over decisions on the rate of taxation paid by multinational corporations to the government of any country. Private bankers and creditors fix the (often usurious) interest rates paid on all loans to domestic individuals and firms. Globalised so-called private equity firms (better defined as *public debt* companies) generate enormous quantities of debt, which they dump on domestic care homes and water companies, for example, and in the event these companies fail, expect taxpayers to clean up the resulting financial mess.

Unlike the imperious governance of earlier emperors, conquerors and robber barons, today's financial governors operate private systems and institutions that are very carefully hidden from public view. The governors do so despite being dependent on state institutions and resources like quantitative easing, subsidies and tax breaks. Global markets like the Chicago Mercantile Exchange that fix the prices of essential commodities, including grains and energy prices, are largely ignored. Yet it was investors and speculators in global markets like the one in Chicago who fixed the prices that led to the 2022–24 cost-of-living crisis in much of the world.

What Is to Be Done?

This book is about seeing, and paying attention to, the international financial and monetary system and its role in accelerating the exploitation of people and the extraction of the earth's precious finite assets. We must base our comprehension and understanding on this simple reality: the globalised financial system is man-made and designed to be remote and unaccountable. Its design is intentional. The ultimate hidden truth of the world, David Graeber wrote, is that it is something that we make and could just as easily make differently. Like the divine right of kings, it is a system that can and will be transformed.[34]

How can we change a system that economists systematically ignore, one whose governors are determined to evade public accountability? First there must be widespread understanding of the international financial system and of the fact it is *designed* and governed to serve the interests of the wealthy – the 1 per cent. Only with that understanding will we be able to organise, to once again redesign the system to serve all of society and the ecosystem.

We know that can be done because it has been transformed before, in the blink of an eye. The system was redesigned, re-regulated and even transformed both before and after the Second World War. And again in 1971 when President Nixon unilaterally, and virtually overnight, dismantled the global Bretton Woods system and launched what came to be known as 'globalisation'.

Another catastrophic global war would inevitably lead to radical change. But we need not accept that inevitability. I believe that with wider understanding, political will and radical action, the system can be transformed and remade.

This book is mainly concerned with the first aim, throwing light on the invisible, globalised financial system, its evolution over the past century and its powerful masters. I then outline the impact of the financial system on pensions, food, energy and housing, as well as on the climate. Finally drawing on the wisdom of economists and historians, I propose ways in which the international financial system can be transformed and made subordinate to the interests of society and the ecosystem.

Scientists and the UN have warned that if human civilisation is to survive, we must cut greenhouse gas emissions and restore stability to the global climate system.

Such a worthy aim is futile and delusional until we, the people, take back control, taming and subordinating the money system to serve the interests of both the biosphere and humanity, not just, as at present, the interests of wealth.

The Origins of Today's 'Revolutionary Situation'

The financial, political and security crises rocking the global economy have deep roots. To understand today's volatility and instability, it is necessary to hark back to the shaky financial market 'structures' (system) built by Wall Street in the 1960s and '70s and triggered by an American president. In fact, it is necessary to go back even further and grasp the importance of imperialism. That is a state of affairs that drives Wall Street and its powerful allies in the globalised financial sector to capture and channel the surplus savings of nations and, under the protection and subsidies of governments, to use force and political power to extract wealth from wherever they can; but especially from heavily indebted, natural-resource-rich, low-income countries.

Today's Global Economic Disorder

Donald Trump won the US presidency decisively in November 2024. He began his second term by disrupting the global trading system and the 'rules-based' international order, while taking a

metaphorical chainsaw to the American federal system and con-
stitution. The world responded with shock and awe.

He was not the first US president to take a wrecking ball to a
rules-based system signed up to by most of the world's nations.
More than fifty years earlier, on 15 August 1971, President Nixon,
speaking on TV, electrified the nation and later the world with
an announcement that proved globally disruptive. He informed
his global audience that the United States would not honour its
obligations to repay debts in gold, as agreed at Bretton Woods.
Thereafter foreign governments could no longer exchange dollars
earned from exports to the US for gold. So, in effect, the international monetary system turned into a fiat one, with the US
dollar dominant. The consequence of Nixon's decision was an
immediate devaluation of the dollar, which made US exports
more competitive.

The United States' allies could not do anything about this
because the US held all the world's reserves (surpluses) in the
vaults of the Federal Reserve. Nixon's declaration led, predictably,
to the unilateral dismantling of the international economic order
of that time, the Bretton Woods system, and to a free-for-all that
resulted in a world of floating, fixed or managed exchange rates.
Since then the global economy has lacked an orderly, stable international monetary system or framework that would ensure states
deal with each other fair and square.[1] Instead, countries were and
are free to build up deficits and surpluses, regardless of the impact
on the world economic system as a whole; and even when such
imbalances raise political tensions.

Along with price and wage controls, President Nixon had, like
Trump, also introduced tariffs to help reduce the US trade deficit
with both Japan and Germany. Plus ça change. Treasury Secretary John Connally had offered Nixon his perspective: 'My
philosophy, Mr President, is that all foreigners are out to screw

us, and it's our job to screw them first.'[2] Four months later Nixon was forced to remove the tariffs. But the harm had been done.

For three days before his TV appearance, President Nixon had secretly consulted a very small group of colleagues at the presidential retreat, Camp David, and had deliberately excluded his own Secretary of State, Henry Kissinger. He was determined to act without the knowledge of allies and international creditors.[3]

The Bretton Woods (BW) economic 'architecture' at which he took aim had been constructed in 1944 thanks to very different, transparent and representative arrangements. An immensely cooperative effort by the world's leading economists (from both North and South)[4] set out precisely to avoid a repetition of the trade and capital account imbalances, and the economic and security crises of the 1920s and '30s. Economic conditions that had led to a catastrophic global war. The BW system was built after a lengthy period of consultation during the Second World War and in preparation for the coming peace. (The British parliament debated the Bretton Woods proposals for changes to the international financial architectures as early as 1943.)

Keynes was alive to the dangers posed to future international trade and finance by the adoption of another hegemonic reserve currency. After all, the dominance of sterling as the world's reserve currency under the gold standard had led to pre–world war tensions and imbalances. In 1941, he began to design an alternative. In 1944, he explained his plan – an International Clearing Union (ICU) – to the House of Lords in one single sentence: 'to provide that money earned by selling goods to one country, can be spent on purchasing the products of another country'.[5]

It was as simple as that.

Keynes's ICU proposal was in essence a trading union based on a banking union. It would enable states to engage in international trade using their own currencies. A surplus or deficit with another state would be managed in much the same way central banks manage the accounts – the daily surpluses and deficits – of commercial, Main Street banks. Countries in deficit would be granted an 'overdraft' but be subject to penalties. But in contrast to banks, countries in surplus would also be subject to penalties if they did not use their positions to trade with others and reduce their surplus. There was, in truth, no need for a currency. The equivalent of the 'central bank' at the heart of country trade transactions would keep an account of surpluses and deficits and would apply penalties to imbalances with the aim of restoring the worldwide balance in international trade.

At the 1944 Bretton Woods conference Keynes wanted to lock the United States into a rules-based international order. The US representative to the conference, Harry Dexter White, insisted on something quite different. The US would not join the clearing union team, preferring to maintain control over its reserves, so that it could lend them out on its own terms. The consequence of American refusal to join in was predictable: the rise and supremacy of the dollar as the world's reserve currency, because as Lord Skidelsky explains, 'in the actual circumstances the dollar alone was convertible into gold'.[6]

While they disagreed over the shared burdens of an international clearing union, White and Keynes agreed strongly on the question of international movements of private capital. Both strongly supported the use of capital controls, writes Eric Helleiner in his magisterial work *States and Reemergence of Global Finance*.[7]

As a result, and despite Wall Street's determination to end capital controls and restore unfettered capital flows, governments retained democratic sovereignty over economic policy for the next two to three decades – the 'golden age' of economics.[8] States were given the explicit right to control capital movements and to manage trade and exchange rates. However, by pegging the world's reserve currency, the US dollar, to a finite supply of gold in Fort Knox, both the American delegation at Bretton Woods and their friends in the orthodox economics profession presaged the collapse of the system under President Nixon. By 1971 and the Nixon TV announcement, the costs of both the Vietnam War and the building of 'The Great Society' had caused the United States to build up a deficit in trade and to empty Fort Knox of its holdings. The US could not redeem its international obligations to repay foreign debts in dollars matched by gold, as agreed at Bretton Woods. In the 1960s, well before the Nixon Shock, French President de Gaulle knew the US had insufficient gold to uphold its promise to convert paper dollars to gold, and ordered the Bank of France to accept US debt repayment only in gold, not greenbacks.[9] In 1971, France's President Pompidou sent a battleship to repatriate gold stored in the vaults of the New York Fed.[10] These accelerating outflows of gold and dollars from the United States to Western Europe in payment for imports prompted Nixon to suspend gold convertibility.[11] Threatened by both the loss of gold and a run on the US dollar, he acted as impetuously as Donald Trump would later do.

At the time, the US default on its international obligations was the biggest-ever such sovereign default, although it is seldom defined as such by economic historians.[12] If the IMF had been called in, the US would have had to adopt a 'structural adjustment' programme to restore balance to its current account and public finances. Given American power and dominance, that was out of the question.

In exchange for the dollar's delinking from gold, the US offered its allies something less tangible as a global standard: US Treasury Bills, or debt. Foreign creditors like the French were invited to hold new loans as a form of collateral guarantee for the money the US owed them. To understand what that means in colloquial terms, I offer this analogy: Joe Bloggs owes you money. Instead of paying, he suggests you make him a new loan (which can be traded in markets and which may or may not rise in value with time) and that you hold that loan as collateral guarantee he will repay in the future. Generous, eh?

Eventually and by default, the US dollar became the hegemonic global reserve currency. The world had moved from the Bretton Woods arrangement to the US dollar standard, with the United States opening up both its trade and capital markets to the world. Cooperative action could not succeed without the US, given the central role Wall Street plays in the global economy and the emerging if chaotic international financial order.[13]

The global US dollar reserve system had deleterious and profoundly unfair impacts on the rest of the world, in particular on low-income countries, as José Antonio Ocampo explains.[14] In a world of imbalances the need to restore balance and adjust economies now falls not on rich, creditor countries but on low-income heavily indebted countries. Furthermore, poor countries fear running out of US dollars with which to purchase basics such as oil and pharmaceuticals, and so build up their foreign exchange reserves by selling more and more of their assets – commodities, manufactured goods and even people – to rich creditor countries. That transfer of a poor nation's human and natural resources to much richer countries is the most iniquitous consequence of the current monetary system.

Nixon's abrupt change to the status of the international system led first to a fall in the value of the dollar, then with time to an inflow of foreign capital into America's open, deregulated capital markets, with the inevitable consequence: the influx of money that poured into Wall Street led to the overvaluation of the US dollar. In the future, a strong dollar would result in global current and capital account imbalances, render US manufactures uncompetitive in world markets and inflate both private and public debt worldwide.

The consequence of the Nixon administration's actions meant that he and his successors presided over the removal of the global financial system's guard rails; the increased mobility of capital (1974); the creation of large, opaque and unbalanced global markets in goods, services and money; and a global, export-led growth model that resulted in the largest, most persistent trade deficits in history.[15] Not to mention the environmental impact of that growth model. And, as van Steenis argues, the Nixon Shock catalysed changes to the way Wall Street did business, with 'the creation of new instruments to bet on the direction of interest rates and hedge currency risk, including Foreign Exchange futures and options'. [16]

Thus began the slow, but inevitable construction of the Global Casino.

The international financial and monetary system began its shift away from a national bank–based system to the global unregulated market-based system that is today's shadow banking. Since then, the world has experienced recurring global financial crises. Unilateral capital controls applied by individual nations could not handle illegal, speculative flows emanating from Wall Street. Flows which proved disruptive of exchange rates and the international trading system. This disruption impacted on the jobs and livelihoods of millions of people across the world. Their loss, pain and suffering were eclipsed by the capital gains being made by the few active in the Global Casino.

Sovereign debt crises began to emerge at the periphery of the global economy – in Africa and Latin America – soon after the Nixon Shock in the 1970s. Debt crises gradually moved to the core – the Anglo-American economies – as I predicted would happen, first in 2003 and again in 2006.[17] By 2007, US subprime mortgage debt, owed by low-income households, was at the base of an inverse pyramid of global public and private debt that towered over it. The subprime sector slowly but surely blew up these debts, culminating in the 2007–9 Global Financial Crisis.

The Nonexistent International Monetary Order and Rising Disorder

After the shock of his 1971 announcement, Nixon and his administration offered no alternative design for the international world order. They strongly opposed cooperative initiatives, pressing for free trade and capital movements. The IMF was invited to propose and construct a new order. Some insist that they tried, but their efforts came to nothing. Instead, Wall Street and the City of London stepped in.[18] There was first a gradual and then rapid deregulation of markets in money and trade, then an end to restraints on cross-border capital flows. The Nixon Shock marked a return to the economic and monetary policies that had underpinned the nineteenth-century gold standard, with gold now replaced by the US dollar.

With time the deregulated structure of the new 'liberal, rules-based global order' sent the value of the dollar soaring, eroding the United States' competitive advantage in manufacturing and leading to both employment and income losses for millions of Americans. What followed was the rise of Wall Street's influence over US economic policy and the evolution of what Oliver Bullough calls 'Moneyland'.

Spurred on by the Chicago School's neoclassical economic policies for the privatisation of public assets, an international system evolved that elevated the political and economic power of private markets, wealthy individuals and firms, and nations with enormous trade surpluses and deficits.

That shift in policies governing money and banking power inevitably had distributional consequences. Trade policies were distorted by the role of the US dollar as the world's reserve currency and its sustained overvaluation, which collapsed manufacturing in the US Rust Belt and, while reducing US production, expanded American consumption of goods and services produced in places like China and Bangladesh. Policies for financial deregulation led to tax evasion; the removal of constraints over interest rates charged by creditors, resulting in high-cost loans and lending for speculation; and the loosening of banking regulation in general. All the while, the rich just got richer.

Since then, the strong US dollar has worsened American trade deficits and boosted China's surplus. It has harmed the interests of low-income countries that are obliged to purchase oil and pharmaceuticals in a currency much stronger than their own. It has inflated unsustainable sovereign, private, corporate and household debt. Ultimately the harm inflicted on the US economy by the 'mighty US dollar' played a big, if unacknowledged, part in Trump's second election victory.

Americans had been warned. Back in 1971, Professor Nicholas Kaldor, the distinguished British economist and adviser to the Labour Government, published an article in *The Times* in which he predicted the inevitable effects of the strong dollar's role on the American economy:

> So long as countries . . . preferred selling more goods even if they received nothing more than bits of paper ('greenbacks') in return, and so long as a reasonable level of prosperity in the US (in terms of employment levels and increases in real income) could be made consistent with the increasing uncompetitiveness of

United States goods in relation to European or Japanese goods, there was no reason why any major participant should wish to disturb these arrangements . . .

But as the products of American industry are increasingly displaced by others, both in American and foreign markets, maintaining prosperity requires ever-rising budgetary and balance-of-payments deficits.

If continued long enough it would involve transforming a nation of creative producers into a community of *rentiers* increasingly living on others, seeking gratification in ever more useless consumption, with all the debilitating effects of the bread and circuses of Imperial Rome.[19]

A French economist, Jacques Rueff, was equally scathing about America's no-cost increased consumption of foreign goods and services, thanks to the privilege of holding the world's reserve currency: 'If I had a tailor, who every time I bought a suit, lent me back the money I paid for it, I would be encouraged to buy far too many suits and might be led into habits of living above my means.'[20]

In fact, millions of Americans were to become victims of the system of deregulated trade and capital markets and of growing income inequality and wealth concentration, as the economist Michael Pettis has explained.[21] The top 10 per cent of the population profited from the system. Their jobs, pensions and inflated housing wealth are sustained by globalisation. The top 1 per cent, the City of London and Wall Street, owe much of their unearned wealth to deregulated and financialised globalisation – 'an international economic regime fully tuned to the demands and wishes of footloose capital'.[22]

Not so for the 90 per cent, including the world's young people.

China's Admission to the System of Globalisation

By the end of the twentieth century, the dogma of 'free trade' supported by capital mobility led inevitably to the China Shock of 2001. China's admission to the World Trade Organization, combined with the US dollar's overvaluation and asymmetric trade conditions, resulted both in floods of capital into the United States and in flows of American investment into China (think Apple, Tesla and Nvidia). The US trade deficit rose from $70 billion in 1993, just before the WTO agreement, to $900 billion in 2024.[23] The admission of China into the WTO led to the loss of US jobs, claimed President Trump and his advisers.

Simultaneously in China, consumption, wages and incomes, especially in rural areas, were depressed, and public and private investment was geared towards the 1 per cent, or those active in the profitable export sector that earned foreign exchange – that is, US dollars.

Nations intent on winning the international war for markets in manufacturing provide subsidies and tax breaks to exporters while presiding over falls in real levels of domestic investment, incomes and consumption. To put it more simply, China and Germany run trade surpluses because of the underconsumption of the domestic economy's production by its people. Underconsumption follows from the maldistribution of wealth and wages and ultimately translates as overproduction. That is because a country's total production is either consumed at home, invested at home, or exported as a trade surplus. In economic terms these two countries face an overproduction problem and a shortfall in domestic demand for what is produced.

As a result, a gulf of inequality opened up between the export and domestic sectors of economies as diverse as China's and Germany's. At the same time, the real incomes of the rest of the population were deliberately repressed or allowed to stagnate (think Germany's Hartz IV reforms that cut unemployment benefit for the long-term unemployed and reduced real wages[24]). That in turn worsened inequality between nations, making export-oriented, surplus-generating economies dominant while trade-deficit countries built up high levels of debt – necessary to fill income gaps and finance imports.

The imbalance between countries with a trade surplus and those burdened by a trade deficit naturally led to a rise in political tensions.

Furthermore, the export orientation of almost all of the world's richest economies had an environmental impact. It led to the build-up of gluts. At an aggregate level, thinking of the global economy as a whole, the overproduction of commodities and manufacturing leads inevitably to record surpluses of 'stuff': overproduction that cannot be consumed. As austerity policies began to bite after 2010, contracting the social wage even as real wages stagnated, wealth expanded relentlessly.

Britain's is an economy where production has stagnated under the international system, with very low levels of investment leading to a chronic trade deficit. Nevertheless, and thanks to the activities of the City of London, wealth for the 1 per cent in Britain has soared. By contrast, wages have stagnated. 'The [British] economy and pay were in an unending doom loop of decline,' Geoff Tily of Britain's TUC argues.[25]

Underconsumption and Weakened Purchasing Power

At a global level, underconsumption of total aggregate production was the consequence. Contrary to much commentary by 'green' advocates, it is overproduction not excess consumption that causes harm to the ecosystem. Most of the world's citizens, dubbed 'consumers', are struggling just to survive. In contrast to the top 10 per cent of the population, the 90 per cent spend all their income on vital services: buying or renting a roof over their heads and on purchasing food, maintaining health and providing higher education for their children.

Far from society's purchasing power chasing too few goods and services, too many goods and services chase shrinking purchasing power. That leads to high levels of debt, as the 90 per cent borrow to finance a home, pay for health and education services and so on, and as firms borrow because sales fall and they can't sell all they produce.

The global financial crisis and subsequent conditions are wrongly judged as the public living beyond the means of the economy. Instead, the economy has operated beyond the means of the public, as Tily notes.[26] Supply is excessive given deficient demand, not the other way round.

These conditions, as we know from experience, led to global financial crises, but also ecological crises. As the European parliamentarian Philippe Lamberts said to thousands of citizens attending an EU conference on climate in 2023: 'This is a fight. A struggle. Even a war – to defend the planet.'

Private Governance of the Global Economy

The supposedly 'apolitical' transfer of public, political and economic power to private interests after 1971 led ultimately to a 'liberal, rules-based' international economic order that looked very much like the imperialism of the nineteenth century but came to be known as 'globalisation'. Economies, except China and its allies, were increasingly governed by a system of private deregulated financial markets in money, commodities and currencies.

The outcome after fifty years was expansion in the size and scale of markets, growth in innovation and the development of new technologies, and worsening trade imbalances as states and corporations competed for markets and for deregulated credit/ finance. Trade imbalances were made worse by erratic private flows of capital into and out of national economies. Speculation by private financiers could cause a nation's currency, or its essential commodities, to rise and fall and thereby destabilise domestic management of the economy.

The intense global competition by states for dominance in export markets and for supplies of credit in capital markets led to greater insecurity and inequality everywhere and to the rise of trade wars, class wars, authoritarianism and even fascism – political phenomena not unlike the tensions and uprisings that had defined the 1920s and 1930s.

After the Dismantling of Bretton Woods

The Nixon Shock of 1971, as Keynes would have predicted, laid the foundations for the Trump Shock of 2025. After 1971, a 'non-system' evolved quickly thanks to the finance sector's collusion with pliant states and to the corruption of politicians. It has with time led to the creation of trillions of dollars of private, unregulated credit that enriched the already rich, burdened millions with costly debt and resulted in low levels of secure, well-paid employment. Those policies embedded historically unprecedented levels of inequality within and between countries.

At the heart of the system was 'easy money', unregulated if expensive credit that can be likened to a global spigot. Credit was used to fuel levels of production that could not be consumed and to undertake levels of speculation, production and extraction that accelerated the climate crisis.

Hyperglobalisation elevated the power of private, global markets over the lives of individuals, while undermining the public, democratic authority of states. It led to what Susan Strange called the 'deterritorialisation' of commercial power – corporations, like those based in Silicon Valley, that seek to operate above and beyond the territories and democratic rule of states.[27]

This system has embedded a sense of despair and insecurity in millions of people. It has burdened governments across the world with unpayable debts and trade imbalances. This system is dominated by private markets in money that made borrowing usurious and led to high levels of private and public debt: markets in property (land) that made it unaffordable for citizens to gain a roof over their heads. Markets in labour that ended job security and lowered incomes. Markets in health and education that denied millions of people access to decent, affordable healthcare and higher education. Markets that triggered strong political reactions worldwide and led to the degradation of land, seas and forests.[28]

As with the gold standard, the defence of unfettered capital mobility and control of inflation became the West's dominant economic preoccupation, together with the work of orthodox economists in both universities and government departments that promoted supply-side economic theory for expanding credit, lowering taxes and removing constraints over trade and capital flows.

These policies were imposed by a global corporate elite – networks of private actors in financial corporations, university departments of economics, in central banks and in non-bank institutions like accounting and law firms, industry associations and credit rating firms. These private actors – a powerful 'mercatocracy', Claire Cutler explained – built up global financial and knowledge structures that promoted the language of 'rational expectations', 'sound monetary policy', 'fiscal discipline' and 'economic fundamentals' imbued with 'neutrality and virtue'.[29] The 'mercatocracy' treated these economic policies and ideas as if they were natural and beyond contention or public debate. These policies came to be defined as orthodox economics.

The Global Casino as Imperialism

The United States, Britain and Europe are home to some of the most powerful of the world's oligarchs. That is not an accident. Britain modelled, shaped and pioneered imperialism, both the colonial imperialism of the nineteenth and twentieth centuries, but also today's dominant economic model of financial imperialism. As noted above, J. A. Hobson (1858–1940) explained the central problems facing Britain and America at that time as political and economic systems that 'placed large surplus savings in the hands of a plutocracy'.[30]

This is how the system worked. As wages and incomes were lowered at home, Britons consumed fewer of the goods produced. This led to a rise in the rate of savings. (Savings are just the difference between total production and total consumption, so that if consumption falls, savings rise.) As the wealthy (the City of London) captured a large slice of those savings, they too were unable to use their rising wealth to consume all the goods and services produced. In other words, there were limits to the luxuries the rich could purchase with their wealth. Underconsumption of the country's production led to surpluses, as firms failed to find consumers and outlets for goods produced. That in turn led to recessions. The only answer appeared to be to find other foreign outlets for both production and savings.

However, foreign investment meant earning the necessary foreign exchange to invest abroad – which required an increase in the production of exports. Hobson explained how the enthusiasm for colonialist expansion could be understood as the need for capitalists to find new foreign markets in which to invest their nation's excess production and savings. It is this economic condition of affairs, wrote Hobson, 'that forms the taproot of imperialism'.[31]

Armed with financing provided by powerful bankers in the City of London on the one hand, and under the protection of a government that used force and political power to open colonial markets on the other, imperialists extracted, exploited and accumulated the fabulous mineral wealth of countries in Africa and of India.

If the wealth and surplus of Britain's imperialists had instead been invested in home markets, consumption would have kept pace with production, and there would be 'no excess of goods or capital clamorous to use imperialism in order to find markets'.[32]

Today, the domestic economic policies of Anglo-American countries include public subsidies, cheap credit and tax breaks that favour the City of London, those active in the export sector and the super-rich. Public financial support generates surplus savings and 'excess consumption' for these sectors and for the rich – who, in the words of Hobson, are as a result in possession of incomes and wealth far in excess of 'the demands of any craving known to them'.[33]

The problem for the 1 per cent – the super-rich – is this: there are limits to the number of superyachts, private jets and big houses they can buy. This leaves them with surplus unspent savings for investments and speculation in foreign markets, where land is cheaper, wages lower and profits higher. Today's plutocracy ('rentiers') prefer to invest effortlessly in financial assets – liquid, intangible assets like stocks, debt (bonds) and securities that entitle the speculator to future payments ('rent') – that do not require any messy engagement either with land (in the broadest sense of the word) or labour.

The City of London, Frankfurt and Wall Street are today awash with plutocrats while the world is awash with countries like South Africa that, despite the transfer of political power to an ANC government, remain 'colonised' by today's financial imperialism.

The 'Revolutionary Situation'

By the 2008 Global Financial Crisis, globalisation in its new iteration as hyperglobalisation had come to a standstill, as Wolfgang Streeck explains in his book *Taking Back Control?*[34] The centralisation of the global political economy by way of simultaneous deregulation of national political economies was an extension, he argues, of the American model to the world. But there was growing resistance to the submersion of national economies and the replacement of national state sovereignty with supranational global governance. By 2025, that international economic order – hyperglobalisation – was fragmenting as the trade policies of countries became more protectionist.

Only the globalised financial system, the power of its elites over deregulated credit creation and the mighty US dollar were, at the time of writing, untouched by the 2025 vandalism of President Trump and his ally, the billionaire Elon Musk. US policies demanding protection (tariffs) for markets in commodities and manufactures (silicone chips, soybeans and autos) while leaving US markets in capital wide open to foreign investors is why Trump's trade war could not create the effects that the 77 million Americans who had voted for him hoped for.

But the American revolt against the international system is

echoed worldwide. In a largely spontaneous and simultaneous global movement against hyperglobalisation, millions of people across the world – from Brazil to Russia, from Texas to Turkey, from Italy to India – are turning to and voting for right-wing strongmen and women like Narendra Modi of India, Jair Bolsonaro of Brazil, Viktor Orbán of Hungary, and Giorgia Meloni of Italy. All promised effectively to take back control and, in the case of Donald Trump, to build walls and impose tariffs to protect workers from the job-wrecking nature of the international economic system. Their arrival on the political stage coincided with the worldwide collapse of social democracy. 'Centrist' politicians were punished for their collusion with financial elites, their commitment to the ultra-liberalism of globalisation and their failure to defend the livelihoods of working people and tackle inequality.

The nationalist and even fascist leaders who replaced social democrats and who have taken power under false pretences across the world are inward-looking and internationally sectarian. Keen to repress democracy at home, they have no strategy for transforming the system. Above all they are nationalistic and divisive, unwilling to unite with allies to tackle the imperialism of the Global Casino. The situation recalled Vladimir Lenin's definition of a 'revolutionary situation': 'when the "lower classes" do not want to live in the old way and the "upper classes" cannot carry on in the old way'.[35]

Yet this revolutionary situation differed from earlier times in one dramatic and radical respect: humanity is now confronted by the grave threat of climate breakdown and biodiversity collapse. In 2021, eleven hundred scientists warned that 'planet Earth is facing a climate emergency'.[36] Human civilisation faces a grave and mounting threat of heat waves, droughts and floods that are driving mass mortalities in species such as trees and corals and exposing millions of people to acute food and water insecurity. Weather extremes have cascading impacts that are difficult for societies to manage.

As human societies we need to conduct ourselves less stupidly than past civilisations, whose inflexibility in the face of climate change led to total collapse, as a group of archaeologists reported in 2014. Having excavated the remains of past civilisations, they very rarely found any evidence of a whole society making attempts to change in the face of a drying climate, warming atmosphere or other changes.[37]

We must develop policies to ensure that society can tackle the security threat of ecosystem collapse, inequality and injustice; that credit is democratised and made available and affordable for productive, sustainable activity and public welfare; that international relations are harmonised and trade stabilised and that Wall Street and other members of the Global Casino are tamed, their activities subordinated to the interests of society.

To behave less stupidly than our ancestors, we need to exercise political power. To understand the simple truth that there are more of us than there are of them. To begin to develop alternatives to the current international financial system; alternatives that can become a matter of public knowledge and understanding and can drive political and economic transformation.

But first we need to go back to basics and understand money.

2

Money and Power

Today, at the end of the century, the casino nature of the financial system has been widely acknowledged. And what we have today is much more of the same – more volatility, more uncertainty and more anxiety . . .

Money has indeed gone mad.

Susan Strange, *Mad Money*

The victory of fascism was made practically unavoidable by the liberals' obstruction of any reform involving planning, regulation, or control.

Karl Polanyi, *The Great Transformation*

This chapter explores how simple, if flawed, economic ideas for the deregulation of money have powered speculation in the Global Casino. These ideas are at the root of the marketisation of the social construct and of the public good that is money and society's money systems. This public good was developed by society over centuries of history to enable us to do what we can do, to echo Keynes. Like public systems of sanitation, clean air and water, the monetary system, if managed well, can enable societies to cooperate and coordinate – to do what we can do – within the limits of the biosphere. And only if it is managed well.

By contrast, today's flawed ideas, theories and policies in relation to money have deep roots in 'classical' economic thought that, despite its many contradictions, remains influential. After the deliberate breakdown of the managed Bretton Woods system in 1971, old, outdated ideas about money were revived, which once again led to recurring financial and economic crises, to the privatisation of the public monetary system, to deregulated financial and trade globalisation and to obscene levels of inequality worldwide.[1]

In short, these ideas for deregulation unleashed capital against democracy.[2] By doing so, they fuelled inequality and financial instability and triggered the reactions of populism, nationalism and authoritarianism. The system of deregulated flows of capital and trade is breaking down, threatening chaos, insecurity and even war.

To change the world, we must first change our minds – and our monetary systems.

The 'Mad Money' That Is Crypto

In September 2024, as he campaigned to win the world's most politically powerful office, Donald Trump vowed to make America 'the world capital of crypto and Bitcoin'. His campaign was helped by the political action committee Fairshake, which spent $173 million to elect pro-crypto candidates from both major parties.[3]

True to his word, on the eve of his inauguration Trump and his wife expressed confidence in crypto by releasing digital memes – $TRUMP & $MELANIA – that are reported to have added millions of dollars to their combined fortune. By doing so the president helped fuel a speculative mania. Bitcoin surged from about $70,000 before the election to a record high of more than $100,000.[4] The only prominent dissident to air concern in public over President Trump's endorsement of crypto was Wall Street billionaire Paul Singer, founder of 'vulture fund' Elliott Management. His company warned in a press release that the 'inevitable collapse' of the crypto bubble 'could wreak havoc in ways we cannot yet anticipate'.[5]

Within two days of taking office, and thanks to the 'mad money' that is crypto, the US presidency had already become more lucrative for Donald Trump than for any president in American history, according to the senior editor of *Forbes* magazine.[6]

Three days after taking office, Trump signed a ready-made executive order with a grand title ('Strengthening American Leadership in Digital Financial Technology') designed to 'support the responsible growth and use of digital assets, blockchain technology, and related technologies across all sectors of the economy'.[7]

Joining Trump at the pinnacle of American power in 2025 were crypto billionaires, Wall Street billionaires and Silicon Valley billionaires. They had all dutifully submitted to the power of the US president and had coalesced, as Professor Jackson noted, around an 'open, ruthless project of class despotism'.[8]

Why would an elected American president set out to undermine the credibility of the world's reserve currency – the US dollar – in favour of an alternative favoured by criminals, fraudsters and money launderers? This happened without stirring public concern or alarm. How and why had governments, with the exception of China, tolerated and even encouraged the lawlessness of cryptocurrencies?

Above all, how did ideas about money degenerate into the deregulated international financial system of today?

The 'fount and matrix' of this system is the self-regulating market.[9] It has powered the rise of eye-watering wealth for a tiny minority. Wealth has more than doubled since 2019 for the world's five richest men, soaring from $506 billion to over $1.1 trillion.[10] That group includes Elon Musk, who paid a true tax rate in the US of just over 3 per cent between 2014 and 2018, according to an investigation by ProPublica. At the same time, Americans without a college degree experienced a real (inflation-adjusted) decline in their wages between 1980 and 2013 – the period of accelerating globalisation.[11]

To understand why that happened, I will briefly scan the history of money as a commodity as it has evolved over the past two centuries, the theory that underpins the creation of cryptocurrencies and the current market-based system of money.

Crypto, private power and the gold standard

The idea underpinning cryptocurrencies – that money is a commodity – is central to all orthodox or classical monetary theory taught in universities. It permits money to be 'privatised' and traded in 'free', unregulated markets. The aim is to ultimately assert private authority over money, to achieve that by undermining democratic regulatory authority over money and the monetary system, and to depoliticise power struggles over money.

The growth of digital assets like Bitcoin was powered by the theory (or perhaps ideology) that crypto is a commodity, an asset, that like gold can be used as money. As Stefan Eich explains, crypto acts in the mind of its creators as 'a digital analogue to gold'.[12] The operation of the international cryptocurrency system resembles the workings of the nineteenth-century 'gold standard' – the system of global markets in money that prevailed between 1880 and 1931. Like the management of economies under the gold standard, the creation and distribution of cryptocurrencies is governed by *private* players – that is, individual crypto miners and by 'the private market' in cryptocurrencies. Just as with the gold standard, cryptocurrencies operate beyond the reach of state regulators and the law and are moved across borders without encountering friction.

Gold is the scarce metal (or commodity) that orthodox economists once considered a proper standard of monetary value. The gold standard system that operated in Britain from 1717 until 1931, and internationally from 1880 to 1931 (with one or two disruptions), was designed by those with financial interests in the City of London with the express purpose of suppressing inflation and limiting exchange rate volatility. The point was to remove the state's role in fixing the value of the currency and, it was argued, increasing the money supply – and to transfer those powers to private, international markets in currencies and money. David Ricardo, a wealthy Dutch-Portuguese merchant and City of London speculator, was one of the architects of the gold standard system.

Under the standard, a nation's currency was theoretically pegged to the value of gold. The supply of money in the economy depended on the rise and fall of gold bars in the vault of the Bank of England. The point was for gold to set a global market standard that would ensure the City of London used the same exchange rates and had the same price level and money rates (broadly speaking) as Wall Street and other financial centres – even while the economies of these states were very different. 'The whole object was to link rigidly the City and Wall Street', Keynes wrote.[13] London creditors who had lent money to, say, railroad companies in New York or Rio de Janeiro considered it vital that the value of the debt they were owed should not be devalued by inflation or by fluctuating exchange rates.

The gold standard system of government by markets

Under the gold standard, countries were expected to limit the issue of new money so that the amount of paper notes in circulation equalled the amount of gold stored in the vaults of their central bank. Whereas money as credit (or the credit system) had been developed over time to enable societies 'to do what they could do' – make products, grow food and employ workers to do so – the gold standard periodically prohibited states, that is, their central and commercial banks, from increasing the supply of money to stimulate economic activity. Instead, when supplies of gold held by the central bank fell, government institutions were automatically obliged to contract economic activity (investment, employment and consumption) to equal the dead weight of gold bars stored in a central bank's strong room. (Today, the IMF uses similar policies, imposing conditionality and 'structural adjustment' on democratic governments to shift economies to a standard they have set on behalf of international creditors who want debt repayments to take priority over other items of government expenditure.)

Governments were expected to increase the nation's holdings of gold by neglecting the domestic economy and reorientating economies towards international markets in money, goods and services. Then, as now, the export orientation of economies is necessary to ensure countries earn hard currency – particularly sterling then and US dollars now – for the purpose of repaying private and public foreign bankers and creditors and for purchasing vital imports like medicines and oil.

If export sales led to the increase of gold bars credited to the central bank, then the domestic supply of money could expand to stimulate more economic activity at home. If the reverse happened, and gold bars earned from exports fell, the economy was forced to contract to equal the amount of gold in the central bank.

The system is said to have removed power over the money supply from the state, though economists question whether the fixed gold 'cover' relative to bank notes was always honoured. Nevertheless, the central aim of the gold standard was to wrest power away from the state over the issuance of paper money, the pricing of money (interest rates) and the valuation of the currency, and to transfer those powers to private financiers, like David Ricardo, operating in both the money markets of the City of London and Wall Street.

The gold standard system allowed markets in money, goods and labour to control the organisation of economic life, which led many countries to prioritise exports, promote free trade and deregulate capital flows. This in turn led to increased competition between nation states, as each battled to access finance and dominate international export markets and colonies. Tensions developed into 'trade rivalries which disclosed the inability of the gold standard to organize a world economy without putting an undue strain on the national systems', as Karl Polanyi argued.[14]

Within countries the elevation of the interests of exporters over the rest of the domestic economy led to the lowering of incomes and to rises in unemployment for those not active in export sectors, conditions and circumstances Hobson had warned of back in 1902.[15] As the rich were mainly associated with both the finance and export sectors, the priority, subsidies and tax breaks given to exporters and the neglect of workers' interests worsened income inequality at home. Klein and Pettis explain in their 2020 book, *Trade Wars Are Class Wars*, that under an export-orientated trading system, 'regular people' are 'deprived of purchasing power' relative to the wealthy exporters in their midst.[16] That naturally raises tensions, but the public are 'tricked by chauvinists and opportunists into believing that their interests are fundamentally at odds' (with foreigners).

US politicians blame unemployment in America's Rust Belt on the Mexican and Chinese governments, when it was American corporations like Apple that were responsible for shifting production to countries with far lower labour and land costs. Just as in the early twentieth century, today, a conflict between economic classes at home and within the domestic economy is misinterpreted as a series of conflicts between countries with competing interests.

International competition for global markets exacerbated geopolitical tensions during the gold standard era and led to trade wars, which ended ultimately in real wars. Karl Polanyi explained this in 1940:

> Within national frontiers . . . well-being of all civilized nations had been immeasurably increased under the sway of *liberal capitalism*; the balance of power had secured a comparative freedom from long and devastating wars, while the gold standard had become the solid foundation of a vast system of economic cooperation on an almost planetary scale. Although the world was far from perfect, it seemed well on the way towards perfection. Suddenly this unique edifice collapsed.[17]

The gold standard system of capital mobility, exchange rate flexibility and free trade ended with the catastrophe of the First World War, the 1929 stock market crash, the Great Depression, the Russian Revolution and a genocide during the Second World War. In the 1930s, Europe moved relentlessly towards authoritarianism and fascism. Only with the election of President Franklin Delano Roosevelt in 1932 and the rise of left governments in some parts of Europe and New Zealand did a 're-balancing between wealth and work and between countries across a significant part of the world' begin to emerge.[18] Those efforts culminated in the design of a new international economic and financial system, Bretton Woods, in 1945.

Today, the economic theories that support a global economic system of government by deregulated markets in money, goods and services once again mimic the ideology of the gold standard.

Crypto's illusions and delusions

Like gold, cryptocurrencies are 'mined' – in this case, by computer power. Like gold, the supply of crypto coins is meant to be fixed, limited and locked up in a vault or wallet somewhere. Bitcoin is marketed as a currency with a limit of minable coins set at 21 million coins by 2140. According to reports in January 2025, 19 of the 21 million had already been mined, mainly by Americans and Russians. (The Chinese Communist Party banned the mining of crypto in 2021.)

Crypto enthusiasts argue that their system is decentralised, with no middleman (bank) or gatekeeper (regulator) managing the system. Thanks to the security of blockchain technology, cryptocurrencies are allegedly scarce by nature *because* they are created by 'miners' in a decentralised process. In the tortured logic of a *Forbes* columnist, 'the decentralised nature of Bitcoin ensures that no single entity has the power to create more of it out of thin air. Thus, another important characteristic is that Bitcoin's *scarcity* is guaranteed by decentralisation.'[19]

The process of creating cryptocurrencies, it is argued, guarantees anonymity, involves complicated mathematical formulae and ensures 'verification of payments and a record of asset ownership that's (nearly) impossible to alter by fraudulent activity'.[20]

Whatever the method and technological process, the fact is that 'scarcity' is a key characteristic of both cryptocurrencies and precious metals like gold – a quality that makes both valuable as speculative assets. Bitcoin's value is maintained because its supply is restricted.[21] For crypto enthusiasts that is the point: the decentralisation and anonymity of private money creation inside a technology (blockchain) means that the power of democratic (political) regulatory control over money creation is removed. Instead that power is bestowed (decentralised) on private individuals.

But crypto advocates have one big blind spot: the imperative to privatise currencies and remove political control over money creation is itself a 'supremely political act that raises profound questions of legitimacy', as Stefan Eich argues.[22]

Money as a Scarce Commodity

Cryptomania did not emerge from within an intellectual vacuum. Those who jumped on crypto founder Satoshi Nakamoto's bandwagon in 2008 drank from a deep well of ideas about money, ideas dating back to Aristotle. Ideas that constantly revive and sustain the concept of money as a scarce commodity, the supply of which can be controlled by private authority.

Those ideas were not dislodged by the 2007–9 Global Financial Crisis despite the world's central bankers' issuance of trillions of dollars of liquidity under the policy known as quantitative easing.

The conviction that money is a commodity or like a commodity – that it is finite in quantity, and that to be distributed efficiently it must be subject to 'the market process' – is a conviction deeply embedded in mainstream economic thought, even among economists who would deny that money is commodity-like. But denials cannot erase evidence embedded in 'classical' or orthodox economic language. Phrases like the price of money (interest) is subject to the 'supply and demand' of and for the 'thing' that is money imply that money is a commodity. Economists discuss quantities of money as a thing that can add up to 'stock' of capital, with 'flows' of money 'circulating' with varying degrees of 'velocity'.

These ideas drive government treasuries around the world to act as if money, like gold or cinnamon, can be scarce, despite evidence to the contrary. They lead central bankers, politicians and technocrats to proclaim, 'There is no money.' The belief in money as a scarce commodity leads all three, on the one hand, to issue trillions of dollars of new money to bail out reckless financial speculators (individuals and institutions) on Wall Street and in other financial centres. And, on the other, they assert there is a shortage of money and that therefore austerity for the wider public, including those who lost their homes in the subprime crisis of 2007–9, is a necessity. These policies unsurprisingly have stirred political uprisings and inflamed populism.

Yet, despite much academic huffing and puffing and the blatant criminality of crypto, these beliefs (dressed up as economic theory) remain deeply entrenched in the economics of international financial institutions, particularly the IMF, central banks, government finance ministries and the economics departments of universities like Cambridge and the London School of Economics.

Hayek and the 'de-nationalisation' of money

The idea of money as a scarce commodity is given greater impetus by what the Institute for Economic Affairs calls Friedrich August Hayek's 1976 'masterpiece', *Denationalisation of Money*. In that publication Hayek argued that the cause of unemployment was not capitalism. Rather it was 'governments denying enterprise *the right to produce good money*'.[23]

Hayek believed that inflation persisted because of state intervention in the valuation of currency and money and because 'money was excluded' from 'itself being regulated by *the market *process*' (emphasis added).[24] In other words, nothing could be allowed to inhibit the development of a private market in the creation, supply and distribution of money.

He proposed to replace the state's fiat money with the establishment of 'several different currencies' that should be 'allowed freely to compete without the interference of government'. Although Hayek did not tie these unregulated currencies to gold, he believed there would always be one currency 'that would keep its value constant in step with the aggregate price of a bundle of widely used commodities'.[25] In the absence of state regulation, this link to a bundle of commodities would allow the *market* to stabilise the value of the dominant currency and constrain its supply.

A wrong-headed idea persists

John Maynard Keynes once rightly noted that 'the ideas of economists and political philosophers, both when they are right and when they are wrong, are more powerful than is commonly understood . . . Practical men, who believe themselves to be quite exempt from any intellectual influences, are usually slaves of some defunct economist.'[26]

To believe that money-as-commodity is a 'defunct' idea, applicable only to crypto and not to be taken seriously, would be to misunderstand why the idea is 'more powerful than is commonly understood'. The power and purpose behind the concept of money as a commodity is this: if money is comparable to commodities like lumber or platinum, then it is but one short logical step to the belief that *trading money in markets* is acceptable. Not just local or national markets, but global markets.

In other words, the apparent misapprehension that money is a commodity allows its advocates to do something impossible for those who understand money as *a social and societal relationship*, a promise to pay. If economists implicitly accept that money is a commodity, then it follows that money *can* be bought and sold in markets. The reasoning goes further: as with lumber or platinum, there can be shortages or gluts of money. If a shortage in the 'supply' of money occurs and impoverishes millions of people, then blame can be laid on an inhuman, invisible, depoliticised institution: 'the market', or 'the gold standard'.

That is how the dogma of money-as-commodity elides the truth. The rise in the concentration of wealth in a few hands begins as an idea, one that leads to greater *private* political power over the creation, pricing, distribution and marketing of money. It culminates in the vulgar levels of inequality we witness across the world today.

It is dogma that permits and encourages the imposition of privately arranged high, real rates of interest – rates of return – on loans or investments made across the spectrum of lending. One that permits loans to be issued at abusive rates of interest. These loans almost effortlessly enrich the lender and take advantage of the misfortunes of others. Today's money lenders and loan sharks are redeemed of the sin of usury by the theory of money as a commodity because, it is argued, *it is not creditors that raise rates, it's the market*. This is how a sin condemned by the world's great Abrahamic faiths and by Buddhists throughout recorded history is conveniently vaporised.

Mobile capital's secret, criminal offshore world
It gets worse. The ideology that underpins the money-as-commodity belief insists there can be cross-border free trade in the buying, selling and marketing of money or capital – just as there is free trade in markets for lumber and platinum. Cross-border flows in money, argue orthodox economists, must be unfettered by any form of oversight or regulation if global

markets in money are to reflect the right price (that is, rate of interest) on money and exchange rates, and if governments, firms and institutions are to compete effectively for the world's apparently limited supply of capital. Trade flows in commodities and services face friction in the form of regulation at borders like those of the European Union, the United States or China. And international travellers face border controls entering foreign domains. Neither trade nor travellers cross borders with the speed and ease demanded by, and granted to, those who own technologically advanced cross-border flows of capital.

That power – a virtually effortless digital global market in money – is what has empowered Wall Street and Silicon Valley plutocrats to transform and destroy home markets and to exploit globally deregulated markets. Capital mobility enables Silicon Valley to profit from exporting American jobs to China, where low-paid, deregulated labour makes products to sell at a higher price into Western markets.

Dodging Taxation

Capital mobility enables multinational corporations like Apple and Amazon to avoid taxation and financial regulation and to operate in secrecy. It gives big companies 'a chance to shrug off laws and rules of other jurisdictions, the countries where most of the world lives', as Nick Shaxson writes.[27] In 2021, the world lost $144.8 billion in tax revenues to tax abuse related to offshore financial wealth.[28] Despite some progress achieved by automatic information exchange, the amount of estimated undeclared offshore wealth remains high, at around $13 trillion (or 9 per cent of global GDP), according to the State of Tax Justice 2024 report.[29] Capital mobility, coupled with the threat to withhold capital flows and investment, enabled billionaires to use their financial power to strong-arm and defeat the financial and taxation regulators of democratic governments.

The ability to move capital across the world at lightning speed is largely thanks to technology that, as Susan Strange explained in 1998, has changed the world's structures of power – both the financial structure and the production structure – by shifting power over trade and production from governments to firms.[30] And it is firms, especially private financial firms, that have developed new technologies that have in turn changed the knowledge structure. According to Strange, 'in the post-war decades and for much of the Cold War, technology was led and directed by states. By the 1990s, it was led and directed from the private sector.'[31]

Dirty Money

Perhaps the most disturbing aspect of deregulated mobile capital is the involvement of organised crime in the international financial system. There have always been criminals involved in international finance, but, as Strange once argued, organised crime is different:

> Large, rich transnational networks flushed with profit from the international trade in drugs, arms and illegal immigrants emerged during the 1980s as big players in international finance. Their operations were the basis for a boom in the business of money laundering – the conversion of dirty money derived from crime into untraceable, legitimate investment funds. Because organised crime has developed from mafias, especially the US and Italian mafias, it has not functioned like other economic enterprises. Secrecy between its members has protected it from state authority. The obligation not to bear witness against fellow

members – the principle of omerta – protected the Sicilians against prosecution until in 1993 the Italian law was changed, making membership a criminal offence.[32]

The Shadowy World of Market Extremism

Hayek's dream of denationalised money is given expression in the most extreme market of all, the unregulated $239 trillion market in money – a system of banking known as 'market-based finance'. This globalised market exists, metaphorically speaking, in the dark space that is the mesosphere – the layer of the earth's atmosphere above the stratosphere. It was famously dubbed 'shadow banking' by economist Paul McCulley in 2007 and is an unregulated system of money lending that by 2007 had created 'explosive growth in leverage and liquidity risk outside the purview of the Federal Reserve'.[33]

The 'shadow' refers to a parallel space (parallel to the earthbound and regulated banking sector) made up of 'the whole alphabet soup of levered up non-bank investment conduits, vehicles and structures,' to quote McCulley. In other words, these are activities – the creation of money, the pricing of money (interest), the lending and borrowing of money – undertaken outside the scope of regulatory supervision. All those transactions add up to a gargantuan market.

Yet, while apparently detached from regulated commercial banks that help finance activity in the economy, shadow banks are also tethered to the world's 'main street' (that is, local) banks and, in that way, pose risks to us all. Economists John Levin and Antoine Malfroy-Camine assessed the sector's 'complex web of interdependencies' between banks and both private equity sector and opaque private credit firms active in 'the shadows'.[34] They reckoned that in 2023, traditional banks in their sample had extended $300 billion, or 14 per cent of their total lending, to those funds. In absolute nominal terms, big US banks have raised their lending to private capital firms approximately 30 times over, from about $10 billion in 2013 to $300 billion in 2023.

The total global financial assets held by shadow banks at the end of 2023 amounted to a staggering $238.8 trillion – more than twice the global GDP (income) of $100 trillion. That was 49 per cent of the world's total financial assets of $486.4 trillion, 51 per cent of which are held in regulated commercial and central banks. And shadow banking is expanding. The Financial Stability Board (FSB) calculated that in 2023 the size of the sector had increased by 8.5 per cent, 'more than double the pace of (regulated) banking sector growth (3.3%)', raising the shadow banking share of total global financial assets to 49.1 per cent.[35]

After the Global Financial Crisis had been triggered by a run on shadow banks, world leaders set up the FSB in 2009 to 'monitor', but importantly, not regulate, 'market-based finance'. The FSB shuns the term *shadow banking* and prefers the technocratic appellation *non-bank financial intermediation* (NBFI).

Shadow bankers do not engage in traditional forms of relationship banking. Instead, they create shadow money (credit and liquidity) for clients (big Wall Street institutions like asset management funds, hedge funds, private equity firms and investment banks). These take the form of promises to repay, backed by tradeable collateral.[36] Yet while shadow bankers act as bankers and use collateral to guarantee that shadow money issued to investors and speculators can be got back in the event of default, they lack the usual safeguards granted to commercial banks. Without access to central bank regulatory frameworks, backstops or discount windows, or to the deposit insurance and other safety nets provided by the state, shadow bankers face grave risks and are vulnerable to panics and runs on the system.

The two most catastrophic runs triggered the Global Financial Crisis of 2007–9 and the COVID-19 great financial crisis of 2020. On both occasions the state, to avoid the systemic failure of the global financial system, was forced to bail out Wall Street and other institutions that had borrowed (leveraged) huge amounts of shadow money against assets (like subprime mortgages) that had collapsed in value. When bankers demanded restitution, borrowers started selling assets to raise cash, but the more they sold, the more prices fell. That spread panic and led to all assets falling in value. Had the world's central banks not pumped massive amounts of liquidity into the money markets in the summer of 2007, we would all have lost access to our bank accounts.

According to the Committee for a Responsible Federal Budget, the US Federal Reserve spent $4.06 trillion between 2020 and 2022 on purchasing assets to bail out Wall Street's shadow banking debtors.[37] The assets had been used as collateral in the shadow banking system to leverage (extend by borrowing) additional finance for investors. Their values collapsed under the strain of the COVID-19 crisis. Shadow bankers, realising the collateral they owned was losing value and therefore could not be used to raise the necessary cash, demanded debt repayment in full, but overextended Wall Street institutions could not meet the repayments.

The Fed stepped in and, in addition to the $4.06 trillion in asset purchases, disbursed $447 billion in 'liquidity measures' for Wall Street, $110 billion on 'other loan purchase programs' and $88 billion on 'lending facilities'. In addition, the Federal Reserve, together with other central banks, dramatically reduced the federal funds rates at which Wall Street could borrow by a total of 1.5 percentage points at its meetings on the 3rd and 15th of March 2020.[38] Interest rates – for those Wall Street institutions eligible to borrow from the Fed – fell to a range of 0 per cent to 0.25 per cent. In other words, the Fed was effectively paying Wall Street to borrow, just as they had done during the Global Financial Crisis. The Fed maintained these effectively negative rates for two full years, until 2022.

Wall Street and its clients – the 1 per cent – could not believe their luck at being in receipt of that state-backed bonanza. This led to one of history's most lavish spending sprees. More superyachts were sold in 2020 than ever before, with 2021 again breaking sales records, according to experts and brokers at the time.[39] Jeff Bezos, founder of Amazon, saw his wealth jump $13 billion in a single day in July 2020, according to a Bloomberg Billionaires Index.[40] In the same year he bought a superyacht for about $500 million.[41]

How is money created in the shadow banking system?

Shadow banks create money when they create a promise to pay in the future (usually overnight). This promise of liquidity is backed by tradeable collateral, usually government-issued or private sector–issued bonds. The bank, which may hold over $1 trillion in assets, markets its liquid (convertible to cash) short-term assets to, for example, pension and insurance funds that need higher returns than those earned on interest-bearing deposits in bank accounts. The asset, having generated those higher returns, is repurchased the following day by the shadow bank, but at a slightly higher price. The price difference is an implicit overnight interest rate. The party selling the liquid security and repurchasing it is considered a shadow bank because they are willing to repurchase assets *on demand*.

The lenders and borrowers ('market-based finance intermediaries') that operate within the shadow banking system include the whole category of financial institutions: hedge funds, money market funds, structured investment vehicles (SIVs), special-purpose entities (SPEs), exchange-traded funds, private equity funds, sovereign wealth funds, and investment and commercial banks. They are joined by insurance firms, mutual funds, pension funds, payday lending and microloan organisations and currency exchanges.[42]

The role played by collateral or assets in shadow banking

To understand how the global market in money works, we need to follow not just global flows of money between lenders and borrowers, but also the production and use of financial products or assets created by those active in the shadow banking sector.

Collateral is an asset pledged by a borrower, which a creditor acquires if the borrower defaults. An asset or collateral is fundamental to the business of lending. It is used in the shadow banking system in place of regulated trust, as collateral provides a guarantee that in the event of default, the lender can be granted the value of the collateral instead of repayment.

The collateral that underpins the creation of shadow money is made up of financial assets. Unlike property or commodities, financial assets are not physical (apart from the paper on which the bond contract or insurance contract is drafted). They are tradeable, liquid, income-generating assets whose value in the present is calculated on yet-to-be-actualised future income streams. They derive their value from a contract or agreement. An insurance contract's value is in the regular premiums derived from that contract. The value of a pension is in the regular savings or payments made by workers and employers to the managers of the pension fund. Bear in mind that financial assets are also liabilities, because the insurance company will one day have to pay out, and the pension fund manager will one day in the future have to disburse regular pension payments.

The assets include corporate and government bonds (promises to pay). When things are going well, they can be more liquid than tangible assets (like property) because financial assets can more rapidly be turned into cash. Big institutional investors demand *safe, reliable future income-generating assets*. The safest and most reliable assets (bonds or debt in 2025) are those of G7 governments, especially the US and British governments.

The Asset Economy

The shadow banking sector is Hayek's denationalised financial and monetary system. In thinking about this sector, we need to understand that institutions within it are not just using money to fund the lending of capital. As Lysandrou and Nesvetailova explain, there is a stock dimension to their activities that results in the creation of new assets or yield-bearing securities – tangible financial products.[43]

Shadow bankers create new products – synthetic assets – for leveraging additional finance. SPEs and SIVs transform 'things' like subprime mortgages and other loans into higher yielding assets. The best known of these were created in the run-up to the 2007–9 GFC: the toxic collateralised debt obligations (CDOs) that bundled risky and non-risky mortgages together. These 'securities backed by securities backed by loans' were transformed into brand new assets with *higher* future income streams promised and insured by companies like AIG.[44]

The demand for new higher-yielding assets (that is, assets with higher rates of return than sovereign bonds, for example) arose because governments had cut back on spending, and therefore issued less debt or fewer bonds. Under President Clinton, public debt was cut so hard and the budget balanced so assiduously that it caused Wall Street to run out of the most valued asset collateral – US bonds or Treasury Bills – on which the world's financiers built their fortunes. That shortage of public, safe assets created pressure on shadow bankers between 2002 and 2007 to create stocks of new higher-yielding assets, products defined as 'synthetic securitisations'.

Assets and their continuous and accurate valuation are vital to the act of borrowing and leveraging additional finance. Flawed valuations can be disastrous for the system of financial capitalism.

In August 2007, panic struck with the sudden realisation that the value of assets held by the bank BNP Paribas against its massive borrowing may not have been correctly valued (as admitted in a press release). No one was willing to use their liquidity to purchase an asset whose valuation could not be trusted. 'The complete evaporation of liquidity in certain market segments of the US securitization market has made it *impossible to value certain assets fairly* – regardless of their quality or credit rating.'[45]

With just one media notice and an uncertain valuation, valuations everywhere were questioned. As a consequence, the global financial system froze and banks refused to lend to each other because of the uncertainty – although many failed to notice the significance of the event straight away.

Markets in Money Unleash Capital Against Democracy

Based on the flawed but powerful political concept of money as commodity governed by markets, the economics profession and its friends on Wall Street have constructed a vast, boundary-busting, often criminal and now dangerously unstable global financial market in money. One that harbours criminal networks, accelerates rates of inequality and fuels fossil burning, 'growth' and consumption. A system that undermines democratic institutions while enriching oligarchic wealth and encouraging billionaires to act on their libertarian and fascistic ambitions. The system is highly divisive, and just as in the late-nineteenth-century gold standard period, it accelerates the scope for geopolitical tensions, war and catastrophe. While parasitic on taxpayers and the state, the Global Casino simultaneously erodes the state's power of collective organisation and the mobilisation of finance. The effective capture by private interests of the public good that is the monetary resources of central banks – which include quantitative easing and low rates, guarantees against losses and regular bailouts – restricts the resources governments need for undertaking radical climate adaptation and mitigation, and thereby undermines confidence in the state and in democracy.

Wall Street and Silicon Valley–based billionaires have used the unregulated system to gamble and to accumulate unprecedented levels of wealth. When the system imploded in 2007–9 and in March 2020, they were bailed out effectively by taxpayer-backed central banks. In this sense Wall Street and the City of London are parasitic on the state.

American modern-day Croesuses wield financial and political power with breathtaking audacity, despite that dependency. In early 2025, Elon Musk, the world's richest man, was in a position to take control of the United States Treasury with a view, no doubt, of ensuring that even more of the nation's public wealth could be denied to the poor and sickly, and in the form of subsidies and tax breaks siphoned instead into the pockets of US oligarchs.[46]

In other words, the Hayekian private, denationalised market in money empowers the plutocrats of Wall Street and Silicon Valley, accelerates inequality and finances criminals. It has also fuelled political reaction to blatant economic injustice. The public demanded that strongmen provide them with protection from exploitative markets. Those demands led to the rise of protectionist, proto-fascist and totalitarian regimes. Like the nineteenth-century gold standard, global markets in money, land and labour have delivered an economic and social transformation of planetary range.

The system resembles an inverted triangle, a skyscraper of finance inflated by a handful of plutocrats towering over the tiny, fragile planet that is home to humanity and nature. A planet now facing the threat of irreversible climate disaster, while governed by careless and even criminal governments and stuck with economies that lack the monetary tools and resources needed to sustain life on earth and ensure the survival of humanity.

Markets in Money as Utopian

For Karl Polanyi (1886–1964), the social and economic theorist, the idea of an unregulated market in money was utopian. No unregulated market – in either goods, land, labour or money – had ever existed, he argued. In his classic 1944 text, *The Great Transformation*, he explained that 'regulation and markets, in effect, grew up together'.[47]

In the nineteenth century, markets under private authority spread all over the face of the globe and the amount of goods involved grew to unbelievable dimensions. Simultaneously, Polanyi explained,

> a network of measures and policies was integrated into powerful
> institutions designed to check the action of the market relative
> to labour, land and money . . . a deep-seated movement sprang
> into being to resist the pernicious effects of a market-controlled

economy. Society protected itself against the perils inherent in a self-regulating market system.[48]

The market as society's only organising power in the economic sphere leads to the debasement of democratic institutions built up over centuries. The rise of authoritarianism, both at the beginning of the twentieth century and today, reminds us that societies react to the power of such a system by seeking the protection of 'strongmen' from the market's impact on humanity and the biosphere.

Inevitably, Polanyi argued, 'society took measures to protect itself, but whatever measures it took impaired the self-regulation of the market, disorganized industrial life, and thus endangered society in yet another way . . . It was this dilemma which finally disrupted the social organization based on it' and led to one of the deepest crises in history: two catastrophic world wars and global economic failure.[49]

The people of the United States took measures in 2024 to protect themselves from global markets that threatened their livelihoods and security. They elected an authoritarian president who promised to protect them, if necessary by force, from Mexican, Canadian and Chinese markets. However, Trump's 2025 measures, on behalf of the American people, including tariffs on foreign imports, impaired the activities of the world's unregulated markets and disorganised the economic and social life of Americans. The 'protection' promised will in the future endanger American society in yet other ways.

Under the authoritarianism of the 1930s, human society endured one of the deepest crises in history. Today, with the risk to our ecosystem, society faces even graver threats. Are we facing a future in which unregulated markets will, as Polanyi argued, physically destroy humanity and continue to transform our surroundings into a wilderness? Or will humanity recognise the risk before it's too late and organise to transform the system and restore both public authority and regulation over the system and stability?

3

Your Pension and the Asset Economy

The emergence of today's globalised financial architecture did not happen spontaneously. It was planned by orthodox economists and constructed by both state and private actors as well as institutions, national and international. As such it can be deconstructed – as it was in 1933 under President Roosevelt, in 1945 under the Bretton Woods Agreement and in 1971 following the Nixon Shock. The key point to note here as we delve deeper into how the system affects you and your family is this: while today's Global Casino operates out in the stratosphere, where financiers evade democratic oversight and regulation, it is simultaneously tethered to the real economy. This chapter is about how the Global Casino is tied to your pension and to your home and to the pensions and savings of millions of others, as well as what that means for all our futures and our security.

One of the most important pillars of the international financial system was built by the brutal dictatorship of Chile's President Augusto Pinochet in the early 1980s. Its most significant experiment – the privatisation of pensions savings – changed the international world order. That experiment was led by a Chicago-trained economist, José Piñera.[1] Deemed a success, it led UK Prime Minister Margaret Thatcher and US President Ronald Reagan to enthusiastically adopt the privatisation model.

However, in the case of pensions savings, responsibility for the subsequent and massive transfer of wealth from a growing number of individual savers into the hands of private managers of global corporations and their shareholders lies with the field of economics. The capture of the economics profession by the neo-liberal Chicago School in the 1970s led to the adoption of an ideology that promoted financial deregulation, unrestrained cross-border capital flows, 'free' trade and the privatisation of public assets – including pension funds.

These changes in economic theory and policy led invariably to capitalism's escape from the regulatory guard rails of democratic policy-making at the level of the domestic economy. Cut adrift from society's values, rules and laws, the finance sector was empowered to create a new territory for financial speculation, profit-taking and capital gains. To finance that new territory, they were gifted with the world's nest eggs, which built up vast stocks of financial assets. I define that new territory as the Global Casino.

Those financial assets in turn led to the establishment of a new globalised system of banking, known by some as shadow banking. Under the new system, the older policies and institutions of the post-war Bretton Woods international architecture, such as commercial high street banks, the IMF and World Bank, were pushed to the margins; today they constitute a much smaller part of the globalised financial system.

Financial Globalisation and the Transfer of Risk on to Individual Pensioners

As a result of pension privatisation, household savings were, and are, funnelled into the 'vaults' of both private pension funds and asset management companies based on Wall Street and the City of London. Brett Christophers, in his book *Our Lives in Their Portfolios: Why Asset Managers Own the World*, estimates that by 1980, about $100 billion had been transferred to Wall Street corporations. In 2014, the Bank of England estimated that private asset management companies, including the Vanguard Group, BlackRock and State Street Global, had scooped up and managed about $87 trillion of the world's savings (assets) globally.[2] A sum equal to the whole of the world's income that year.

That figure seems high, but by the year 2020, financial assets under management (AUM) had jumped to $100 trillion. By 2023, the total had risen to $112 trillion – $12 trillion more than global income.[3] One hundred and twelve trillion US dollars is an alarmingly large sum of money. The vastness of the sum is what makes it inconceivable to most people. That may also be the reason its existence is often simply denied or ignored by most professional economists as well as politicians and commentators.

The Bank of England's executive director at the time, Andy Haldane, explained in 2014 why the sums of savings in the hands of global private companies had increased dramatically over time. Unsurprisingly it was not down to the skills and foresight of fund managers. It was simply that the pool of prospective global savers had become larger, older and richer. After 1950, average life expectancy had risen by nearly 50 per cent, world population had risen by a factor of three and world GDP per capita had risen by a factor of nearly forty.[4]

Once lodged inside a private asset management corporation, your pension nest egg can be actively invested by managers in highly rated government bonds (debt), to earn interest. Or the funds may be invested in more speculative stocks and shares, currency, property or commodity markets. Quite often pension funds are invested 'passively' by the manager of the fund, simply tracking and investing in a basket of securities (Exchange Traded Funds) that can be traded like stocks and shares.

From the 1980s onwards, there was a concerted worldwide move away from traditional, pay-as-you-go state-administered pension systems in which tax revenues were used to pay pension benefits.[5] Under such defined benefit (DB) pensions, risks are, and were, pooled and collectivised, and benefits defined in advance. They were in effect, publicly guaranteed. With the new privatised defined contribution (DC) pensions, benefits are not defined in advance, and risk and reward shifted on to the individual pensioner, saver or insurance holder.

In the UK, membership of pooled and collectivised pension schemes fell from 31 per cent to 14 per cent between 2008 and 2014. At the same time contributions to the riskier DC funds were roughly twice as large as those to DB schemes. The risk is almost entirely one-sided as the executive director of financial risk at the Bank of England reminded pensioners in 2014:

> Asset managers do not bear credit, market and liquidity risk on their portfolios. Currently, BlackRock has over $4 trillion of assets under management but has only $9 billion of assets of its own. Fluctuations in asset values do not threaten the insolvency of an asset manager as they would a bank. Asset managers are, to a large extent, insolvency-remote.[6]

This means that while companies like BlackRock, acting as agent on behalf of end-investors (i.e. pensions funds), might invest pensions and pension funds in globalised markets, they are not responsible for the investment risk – the fluctuations in the value of investments undertaken on behalf of pension funds. In other words, while fluctuations in investment values may not affect asset managers, they do impact on future payments to individual pensioners and investors. And unlike asset managers, pensioners are not 'insolvency-remote'. When markets downgrade or upgrade the value of an investment, it is the pensioner who makes the gain or bears the risk of future losses.

The transfer of wealth to private corporations, which operate in what is effectively an unregulated stratosphere, means that households are increasingly exposed to global financial markets. As the Bank for International Settlements (the grandaddy of all central banks) explained mildly, 'retirement income is subject to greater variability than before'.[7] This is not only the case in OECD countries but even more so in so-called in emerging markets, where pension reforms adopted a structure predominantly based on DC pension schemes.

To understand why and how billionaire corporations are protected from risk when individual pensioners are not, let's briefly digress into the evolution of today's asset economy. There's a reason spies are known as assets. Informers working for a spy agency are 'owned' by that agency. Similarly owned are those properties we call assets – financial, physical and intellectual, including a fictitious asset, *labour*.

The economy after the Second World War could be divided between those who laboured by hand or brain and lived on income from wages, salaries and labour-based entitlements and those, the relatively richer, who lived on the capital gains (rent) made from property or assets. The owners of assets can make what are effectively effortless, unearned capital gains from their assets. In contrast the 99 per cent earn regular income from their labour. Today, the latter group are finding regular income increasingly precarious, while the numbers of those gaining wealth from the ownership of assets has expanded.

Since 1980, the global economy has undergone dramatic changes, with the globalisation of the labour force, the rise of automation and, above all, the growth of Big Finance, Big Pharma and Big Tech. As the economist Guy Standing has documented, this has led to the rise of the precariat, 'a mass class defined by unstable labour arrangements, lack of identity, and erosion of rights'.[8]

The transformation of labour into an asset – albeit a 'fictitious' asset – is best explained and embodied by the precarious arrangements for employment in the oil and gas industry. For many years workers were employed by a company investing in oil and gas exploration. Both workers and company were domiciled in their home countries. That changed dramatically thanks to taxation policies and globally coordinated financial deregulation. Companies could move away from higher tax regimes to countries that harboured tax havens. There they could employ low-paid foreign workers to undercut workers domiciled in the home country. Alternatively, companies could outsource the employment of workers to contracting agencies. Outsourcing allowed companies to cut wages, pensions and benefits and avoid the 'risk' of taxes, employment law and regulations. One oil rig employee, Matt, explained the changes in a survey conducted by a Scottish social and environmental collective known as Platform.[9]

The company didn't pay the best, but they didn't lay people off, it looked after its staff. But when the company grew, things began to change. You became a number rather than an individual.

Since the IR35 tax break, there's a difference between a

contractor that works for a company and someone who isn't an employee – because the companies don't want the risk. I've gone to agencies who employ contractors as staff and have had to go back as an independent contractor and take a 25% pay cut. This is happening on a wide scale. It's very attractive to companies because they don't have to take on the risks of employees. I fear in the long term that IR35s will allow for companies to get rid of workers whenever they want. They have zero risk. They can take on 150 guys and then get rid of 150 guys 6 months later.

While labour, both domestic and foreign, was being contracted out effectively as precarious 'assets' to be hired and fired, not as employees, things were changing in another part of the economic forest: housing.

The Asset Economy, the Global Casino and Thatcher's Revolution

Mrs Thatcher laid the foundations of today's British housing crisis with her government's policy of granting public sector tenants the 'right to buy' the property they lived in at a discount rate. The policies of the 1980 Housing Act were accompanied by a punitive rule: that the finance raised from sales of publicly owned assets could not be used to build new social housing. Today, the British government pays £9.3 billion a year in housing benefits to private landlords housing poorer tenants on behalf of the state. Tragedies like the burning hulk of Grenfell Tower, where seventy-two tenants died on 14 June 2017, are testament to public regulatory failure to protect Britain's remaining social housing tenants but also to add to the supply of affordable social housing.[10]

Britian's housing shortage reflects a global housing crisis. Many buy a home as a primary residence (owner-occupied), not a financial asset. However, others buy a property as an investment or rental property. The latter includes individual investors or institutional investors like private equity firms. KKR (Kohlberg Kravis Roberts & Co.) is an American global private equity and investment company that in 2025 acquired a £100 million (€116 million) portfolio of three UK build-to-rent properties.[11] Their acquisition of the Slate Yard in Manchester consists of 424 residential units across three properties, totalling 270,000 square feet.

The rise in prices for property assets is worsened by corporations like KKR aiming capital flows at housing markets. Their capital investments inflate the prices of safe, if limited, supplies of investable property assets. That means prices for homes in Britain – like residential properties around the world – are inflated effectively by 'too much money chasing too few' properties. In the end, this makes a home purchase well beyond the reach of those who do not own assets, including millions of young people.

Thanks to financial globalisation, finite supplies of property assets have been transformed into financial assets that generate capital gains, both in the form of rents on property but also from the sale of properties when their value is effortlessly inflated by the very process of financialisation.

Housing, the Global Insurance Industry and Climate Breakdown

Property or real estate assets are reckoned to be the largest asset class in the world. The inflation of property values has simultaneously propelled the expansion and profitability of the global insurance industry.

Insurance is an asset, a financial derivative that depends for its value on the underlying value of a property and on the regular premiums paid by property owners wishing to protect their homes or businesses. The Bank for International Settlements (BIS) explains that 'insurance plays a crucial role for individuals, households and small and medium-sized enterprises', affected by what in insurance lingo is defined as 'NatCat events', shorthand for national catastrophes.

The BIS goes on to argue that insurance offers 'financial protection, aids in recovery and can incentivise risk prevention and reduction. Besides such microeconomic benefits, insurance also contributes to macroeconomic resilience by encouraging disaster preparedness and helping to absorb the negative financial impact on the economy after a NatCat event.'[12]

But while insurance companies may help 'absorb the negative financial impact of a NatCat event', they are also guilty of *causing* instability, as the 2008 collapse of the giant insurance company AIG demonstrated. As climate change increases costs and losses for the insurance industry, these companies' withdrawal from the climate-exposed regions may in itself precipitate a global crisis, as occurred during the subprime property collapse. There can be no doubt that insurance companies will act to avoid the risk of climate breakdown. Indeed, they are already doing so, as the chair of the US Federal Reserve, Jerome Powell, confirmed in evidence to the Senate Banking, Housing and Urban Affairs Committee on 11 February 2025: 'Some areas of the United States may be uninsurable in coming years.' Insurance companies and banks, he said, are already 'pulling out of coastal areas, areas where there are a lot of fires'. He went on to predict that in 'ten or fifteen years there are going to be regions of the country where you can't get a mortgage.'[13]

Such withdrawals by the insurance industry have implications for wider financial stability, as US Senator Whitehouse explained on 6 March 2025 at a Senate confirmation hearing for a Trump Treasury appointee. 'Economic storm clouds on the horizon' caused by climate change were, he said, 'chickens coming home to roost. The place where that is most evident, where an industry is obliged to look truthfully at what the future portends, and not at the fake hoax promoted by the fossil fuel industry' is the insurance industry.[14] In what was a fiery speech, he warned:

> An insurance collapse around coastal property values will cascade into a mortgage collapse around coastal property values, that will cascade into a crash in coastal property values that will be so significant economically, that it will cascade out into the full economy in the same way that the mortgage meltdown in 2008 cascaded out into the entire economy.

The Asset Economy and Taxation

One of the great advantages of asset ownership is lower taxes. Tax on income from labour tends to be higher than tax levied on assets or property. Any attempt to equalise taxes on income earned from property and labour is fiercely resisted by the wealthy, as is the way of the powerful. Equalisation is now also opposed by those who own a property but are not defined as wealthy. By co-opting a whole new class of homeowners into the world of asset ownership, the wealthy have ensured protection from higher taxation.

Lisa Adkins and colleagues explain in their book *The Asset Economy* that when President Carter in 1976 promised to equalise the taxation of capital gains and ordinary income and called for the tax code to become more progressive, 'a Wall Street-driven counter offensive sprang into existence', supported by the orthodox economist Martin Feldstein, who would soon become president of the prestigious National Bureau for Economic Research.[15] The campaign was successful. Since then, respective Republican presidents have both lowered capital gains tax and then, when public debt rose, raised it again.

As in the US, so in the UK. In the 2008 Budget, the Labour Government of Gordon Brown made an unprecedented cut to the general rate of capital gains taxation, which Chancellor of the Exchequer Alistair Darling argued would 'reward investment . . . so we are right to now tax gains at a lower rate than income – and the new single rate is among the most competitive in the world, less than half the top rate for income, and also less than half what it was ten years ago'.[16]

That is the way for powerful owners of assets.

All that Is Solid: The Asset Economy, Fluctuating Values and Crises

Assets can be physical, like property or machinery, or financial, like government or corporate bonds or equity (stocks and shares). Earning regular rents from an *existing asset* – such as a Rembrandt painting or Microsoft software – requires far less effort and risk than the profits to be made from investment in the *creation of new assets*.

Assets are valuable as collateral for leveraging additional finance. Creditors will only lend if they can take possession of a borrower's asset or collateral in order to receive full or even partial payment in case of the borrower's default.[17]

The value of pensions and insurance contracts to big asset management funds derives from the strength (or fragility) of the assets underpinning the fund. Some assets are more valuable and less risky than others. The value of an asset that is an insurance contract derives from the regular premiums paid by individuals and firms on insured property. The value of a pension fund depends on regular contributions by workers and their employers. For stocks and shares the cash flows are dividends paid to the owners of the asset.

Continuous and accurate *valuation of assets* is at the nerve-wracking heart of today's financial capitalism. Flawed valuations can be the cause of systemic crisis – and of losses for investors and pensioners – unless and until we are compelled to face reality. Why so? readers may ask. Karl Marx hinted at an answer in *The Communist Manifesto*. 'All that is solid', he wrote, 'melts into air. All that is holy is profaned, and man is at last compelled to face with sober senses his real conditions of life, and his relations with his kind.'

Present-day financial capitalism, or the asset economy, transforms property, newspapers and magazines, care homes, football clubs, brands, animal pets, doctors' surgeries, forests and works of art (the list is endless, but all can be called assets) into income-generating collateral. They are all assets that can be sold by a creditor to raise cash to pay down outstanding debt defaulted on by the borrower. Today, collateral – like a care home promising to pay fees in the future to the new owner of the care home – is used as collateral against which to raise (leverage) trillions of dollars of additional finance (debt). That is because the existence and ownership of the care home and its promise of a stream of future fees (the collateral) act as guarantee of repayment (or partial repayment) to a creditor lending additional finance to the owner of the care home.

In other words, asset managers use the promise of future returns from assets as collateral against which to borrow more. The quality of collateral is defined by its safety and its liquidity (that is, transferability). For as long as the underlying value of the asset stays the same or even rises, all is well. The key point is this:

the asset has its value in *the present*. But its real value is calculated on the basis of yet-to-be-actualised *future, and therefore uncertain* income streams. And therein lies the rub – and the risk of asset valuations.

When the market's valuation of an asset (say, a care home for the elderly) falls, the debt leveraged against it rises in relative terms. Just as a fall in the value of a property can shift a home-owner into mortgage negative equity, so a fall in the valuation of assets can threaten default by those who have leveraged too much debt against an asset. To avoid eviction when the lender takes possession of the property as partial repayment, the owner of a house is obliged to obtain additional finance in order to repay the debt in full and avoid default. In just the same way, borrowers in the Global Casino are pressured by a fall in the valuation of assets to scramble for additional finance to repay calls by the lender or banker. Alternatively, the owner is forced to sell the asset for cash.

The Woes of the Asset That Is the *Spectator* Magazine

The story of the unexpected bankruptcy and then sale of an influential British magazine can help illuminate the way in which wealthy investors, in this case foreign investors, acquire assets and then use the collateral to leverage additional finance.[18]

Andrew Neil was chairman of the conservative *Spectator*, one of Britain's oldest political magazines – 'established in the age of the quill pen'. He was recently forced to resign after the magazine had been 'placed in receivership' by its bankrupt owner, Frederic Barclay, and sold to a right-wing Christian nationalist.

The way in which he and his team of journalists had been treated by Frederic Barclay angered Mr Neil. They, he asserted in his resignation letter, had borne all the risks associated with publication of the valuable asset that is the *Spectator*. Yet they shared not a penny of the capital gains made from the sale. Flourishing his 'quill', and with just a touch of exaggeration, he lamented the sale of his beloved magazine thus:

> In recent years the *Spectator* has never been more profitable, its reach never wider, at home and abroad (helped by our splendid Australian and American editions) and its journalism (under the peerless Fraser Nelson) never better nor more influential than it has been in its almost 200-year history.[19]

Neil explained that a pertinent indicator of his colleagues' achievements was that a magazine given a notional value of £20 million two decades ago was sold for around £100 million in 2024. At a time, he argues, when most 'legacy' publications are struggling to retain anything like their pre-digital worth, this was an unprecedented increase in value.

It is sad, he wrote, that

> nobody responsible for this success – that is, everybody at 22 Old Queen Street – would share in the upside . . . a result of the strange and surprising circumstances, definitely not of our making, we found ourselves in June 2023.
>
> Suddenly and without warning we were placed in receivership because our then proprietors *had used us as collateral* for massive debts unrelated to us (without ever telling us).
>
> They then failed to pay these debts [emphasis added].

Government Assets and the Global Casino

The value of an asset that is a government (sovereign) bond derives from the regular 'rents' or interest paid on that bond: interest paid by government treasuries. Bonds issued by OECD countries, the 'advanced economies', are regarded as safe assets. The bonds of low-income countries are viewed as much riskier. Lenders who buy and sell government bonds in global financial markets fix interest rates on all sovereign bonds. Low-income countries are charged higher rates of interest by private capital markets on what are perceived as riskier bonds.

Asset management funds, hedge funds and private equity firms buy up and use bonds issued by emerging market economies because the regular flow of rents deliver rates of return that are often higher than interest rates on OECD bonds.

Contrary to much comment, Western economies have largely abandoned the world of industrial capitalism and of profits made by entrepreneurs and risk-takers invested in the creation of new assets. We are living through an age of financial capitalism: an era of hyper-financialisation in which investors prefer the capital gains made from speculation in existing assets – like Bitcoin, London's property market, New York's art market, Chicago's energy market or Silicon Valley's tech markets.

Financial crises occur when defaults loom because property prices fall, confidence in bond markets evaporates or unemployment rises. Such events lead to a fall in cash flows from the asset, a downward revaluation of the underlying asset, and to the rapid rise in the debt leveraged against those assets. For pensioners the crisis manifests itself as a default on future pension payments. For the holders of government bonds, it means a crash in the returns, or interest paid on bonds. In some cases, governments could default on interest payments owed. For the holders of insurance contracts, premiums evaporate.

It's Valuation of the Collateral, Stupid

To understand why the valuation of assets is such a big issue for the private finance sector, remember this: the global financial system froze in August 2007 and then collapsed because of a lack of confidence in the valuation of financial assets.[20]

On 9 August 2007, Reuters reported that BNP Paribas bank was barring investors from redeeming cash. It had suspended activity in three of its funds so it could more precisely assess their value. BNP explained their decision in this way: [21]'The complete evaporation of liquidity in certain market segments of the US securitization market has made it impossible to value certain assets fairly – regardless of their quality or credit rating.'

In other words, the crisis did not erupt because financiers ran out of money. Nor because of a run on the banks. The Global Financial Crisis blew up because everyone in the sector lost confidence in the value of assets used as collateral, particularly the value of subprime property mortgages on the balance sheets of commercial banks like BNP Paribas. If those assets could not be properly valued, then the value of all other assets linked to the sector could not be trusted either. Liquidity – the ease with which an asset can be converted into cash – evaporated, because *trust* in the system of valuing assets had weakened.

That mattered because the value of subprime assets (mortgages) had been used to leverage inordinate amounts of additional finance through borrowing. If the asset or collateral against which the borrowing had been leveraged was worthless, then the leveraged debt was unlikely to be repaid from the sale of the promised subprime collateral. The collapse of confidence in asset values (or collateral) thus led to the collapse of the globalised financial system.

Can Fund Managers Be Trusted with Our Savings?

The world's savings and the security of future pension payments have long been a matter of profound concern. These fears were heightened by the debacle that led to the 2022 resignation of UK Prime Minister Liz Truss and her chancellor, Kwasi Kwarteng: their 'mini budget' of September 2022, with its proposal for large unfunded tax cuts for the rich unsettled bond markets. Holders of bonds (assets) believed the Truss government was going to flood the market by issuing many more bonds. Because of the way the market works, the prices of bonds would fall (as in any market) and the interest on bonds would rise. That would raise the cost of debt or borrowing.

At the time, DB pension funds had lower-than-normal collateral levels against their borrowing. As the bond market tanked and yields rose, pension funds were 'margin-called'. This required them to deposit additional collateral with their lenders to prove that they were safe. Because they lacked the capital to fund those collateral deposits, they began to sell their securities (assets). That process of de-leveraging caused panic, so that yields (returns) on gilts (government bonds that, unlike conventional bonds, are automatically adjusted for inflation) rose even higher, causing a wider group of pension funds to be drawn into a 'doom loop' of bond sales and capital-raising.

As the *Guardian* explained, the Bank of England 'was forced to intervene . . . to stop a "doom loop" in the gilt (bond) market as funds used in the pensions industry to support the retirement schemes of people across the country came close to collapse'.[22] The event reminded the public of the precarity of future pension payments when pension funds dabble in the private, largely unregulated and volatile Global Casino.

On Pensions, Gangsters, Warlords and Mercenaries

In January 2023, the media reported on a sensational court case involving the 2020 collapse of the global payments group Wirecard. The case highlighted the risks faced by investors (savers and pensioners) in lightly regulated global corporations, including asset management companies. The case was complex. At its heart was a missing €1.5 billion ($2.3 billion) and the whereabouts of the company's fugitive chief operating officer, Jan Marsalek, who is now on Interpol's 'most wanted' red list. Marsalek was the apparent mastermind behind the company and was rumoured to be living in 'an elite, gated community in Moscow, Russia, under the direct protection of the Federal Security Service (FSB) government agency'.[23]

One of the *Financial Times*'s most talented investigative journalists, Dan McCrum, had pursued the case over several years, exposing the nature of Wirecard's criminality. He persisted despite fierce intimidation from Wirecard stakeholders by way of their high-powered City of London law firms and asset fund managers.

When McCrum started digging and writing damaging stories about the company in May 2015, Wirecard's market capitalisation was €5 billion. Four years later, on 30 January 2019, as the *FT* prepared to publish another story of how Wirecard was knee-deep in the worst kinds of porn, gambling and online scams, the company's market capitalisation had risen to a staggering €21 billion. The *FT* story had little impact. After publication only €7 billion was wiped off their capitalisation, leaving the valuation of the asset that is Wirecard at a massive €14 billion.

Ten months and many regulatory and legal shenanigans later, with the company's market capitalisation having risen to €19 billion, the *FT* tried again. This time with an Exocet missile of a story. In response, the company's share price did fall, but market capitalisation dropped by only €6 billion, to €13 billion. Thirteen billion euros for a company whose real activities were unknown to its investors, board members and auditors and to all those with stakes in the company!

Later McCrum's 300-page blockbuster *Money Men* was made into an equally gripping Netflix documentary, *Skandal!* McCrum's book was riveting, but even after careful reading, I had still not fully understood how the company's executives made their billions. That, it seems, was the point. Nobody, not its investors, asset managers, media commentators or regulators – the presumed 'guardians of the nation's finances' – really understood what was happening inside Wirecard. Its top brass appeared to be in bed with warlords, spies and mercenaries. Yet the corruption and money laundering was overlooked by the company's auditors, Ernst and Young.

This is a story of lawlessness as a feature of freewheeling financialised capitalism, not a bug. *Money Men* is a tale of how such common or garden malfeasance is taken for granted by many of those in charge of the world's pension savings. The investigative journalist Paul Murphy named and shamed key investors in an *FT* article, 'The Fund Managers Who Kept Faith with Wirecard'.[24] Towards the end of 2022, German journalist Christian Kirchner stumbled across an intriguing fact: one of Germany's leading fund managers had made what he described in the Finanz-Szene newsletter as a 'crazy bet' on Wirecard. DWS pension fund managers had gone on a Wirecard buying spree immediately after the *Financial Times* had published extensive evidence proving that a large portion of the company's revenue and profits did not exist. Fund manager Tim Albrecht and his colleagues had bet more than €500 million of their investors' money that the *FT* reporting was wrong!

German fund managers (and their absentee regulators) were not alone in their irresponsibility. When all was said and done in the protracted case inching its way through Munich courts, the real 'skandal' of the Wirecard story is not the corruption, pornography and warlords. Nor is it the story of a fraudulent, fugitive COO protected by Putin's regime. Rather it is about the threat posed to the world's pensioners, savers and investors by easy mobile money and by reckless asset fund managers, careless regulators and ignorant policy-makers – many of whom are meant to be managing our pensions, premiums and dividends. Most, it seems, are fast asleep at the spinning wheel of the Global Casino.

The Global Casino and the Shadow Banking System

To manage their wealth, and with the implicit support of central bankers and economists, investors, bankers and fund managers siphoned the world's savings into a new institution: a global 'money market'. Unlike the domestic system of banks with a physical presence on high streets, this market for money operates in the financial 'stratosphere', beyond the reach of regulatory democracy. It emerged as a response to a new set of mechanisms – customs, institutions and policies – designed to limit financial instability. The market was established during the 1970s, at the start of what economists call the 'post-Bretton Woods financial globalisation supercycle'.[25]

There was sound reasoning behind the establishment of this invisible global market for money. Thanks to privatisation, asset management funds and big investment banks had been granted custody of trillions of dollars of the world's savings. These could not safely be deposited in high street banks, where governments guarantee only a tiny fraction of the huge amounts held by global corporations. As a result, the world's savings are held, somewhat riskily, in the largely unregulated global money market, managed by private, not public (that is, democratic) authority. A new banking system then developed. One far less tangible and visible than the real-world banking system. A system whose reach is global.

In that system, asset management funds, hedge funds, real estate, infrastructure and commodity funds, private equity and insurance firms, and shadow banks gather together even more of the world's savings, including the savings and profits of corporations and of nations – sovereign wealth funds. Inside this new form of banking, a new system of lending and borrowing has emerged. Money (cash) held by financial institutions is exchanged for collateral in the form of real assets (including bonds) with a promise of repayment over a period of time and at a particular rate of interest (or 'haircut').

This is briefly how it works. First, cash is not an interest-bearing asset. Furthermore, its value is prone to fall in inflationary conditions. To protect the value of cash from inflation, an asset management fund will lend it out to earn interest paid at rates above inflation. The fund may make a temporary loan of cash to another financial institution in exchange for safe collateral and at what is effectively a rate of interest. The borrower promises repayment (or repurchase) of the collateral at a slightly higher price, by a later date or time. The higher price demanded by the lender for *the repurchase* of the asset is the implicit interest rate on the loan. Because the exchange is a temporary loan and repurchase agreement, it is known as a 'repo'.

Repos qualify as money because, like money, they are a promise to trade at par on demand without any loss in value.[26] In good times, repos are considered as safe and as liquid as money. However, when a crisis hits, assets used as collateral against a repo can quickly lose their value. Regular high street banks are protected by publicly regulated safety net structures and the value of money they hold for depositors. No such central bank protection mechanisms exist for the shadow banking system. Because the collateral used in repo markets is not backed by government guarantees, the shadow banking system, as Professor Wullweber argues, is fundamentally unstable.[27]

That is where your pensions may be currently lodged.

Ironically, the private US and European repo markets, the largest money markets in the world, are sustained on the foundation (or 'plumbing') of collateral that is government debt. In other words, OECD government bonds issued to generate finance for the state act as the safest form of collateral, or guarantee against repayment, in the private credit creation system of shadow banking. That safety arises because OECD governments can be trusted to regularly pay interest on the bonds over many years – and to repay the principal.

Public sovereign OECD debt in this private financial system is not treated as an economic problem, as it is in public debates about government spending. Instead, OECD government debt is valued by private finance as a very safe form of collateral, the very cornerstone of today's modern, *private*, market-based financial system. Used as a benchmark for pricing private financial assets, it is invaluable to Wall Street and the City of London. When and if governments cut back on borrowing, such collateral becomes scarce and damages the fundamental plumbing on which the wealth of these private financial centres depend.

To recap: the big *public* sovereign state sustains and obliges the *private* shadow banking system by operating what Professor Daniela Gabor calls a 'collateral factory'. She writes, 'Private credit creation . . . fundamentally relies on the dynamics of sovereign bond markets, the collateral factory for a collateral-intensive financial system.'[28]

However, unlike regulated banks, shadow banks lack access to the liquidity provided by central banks in times of crisis. With calamitous results. For example, in March 2020, the global coronavirus pandemic created panic and stress in the shadow banking system. Investors moved over $100 billion from the system's prime funds into government securities (bonds). As the Federal Reserve Bank of Kansas City explains, 'the flow was unanticipated, abrupt, and disruptive, constituting a run on prime Money Market Funds and a sudden flight to safety.'[29] As in 2007–9, the private system was bailed out in 2020 by the world's most powerful, public central banks.

If your pension savings are held within the walls of the shadow banking system, be warned: shadow banks remain vulnerable to future runs because they lack the safeguards and guarantees available to regulated banks or depository institutions. And there may be a limit to what publicly backed central banks can do to protect your investments.

Financial Guardians Monitor, but Are Reluctant to Regulate

While the new international financial system is largely privatised, there is some limited public oversight of the system. The Financial Stability Board (FSB) was set up by world leaders after the Global Financial Crisis of 2007–9 to monitor the Global Casino. The Board rejects the moniker *shadow banking* and instead defines the activities of the private, unregulated banking system as non-bank financial intermediation (NBFI).

According to the FSB's latest report, global financial assets (cash, stocks, bonds, mutual funds and bank deposits) rose to $486 trillion in 2021.[30] Banks continued to be the largest financial entity type, especially in emerging markets. The shadow banking sector constituted nearly half (47 per cent) of the world's total financial assets. Because of interest rate hikes from 2021 onwards, the value of the sector fell to $217.9 trillion in 2022. Even with that fall, it constituted more than twice the total global income (GDP) from real economic activity.

Why does all this matter to you and me, members of the world's citizenry? This wall of money managed by Wall Street and other private financial entrepots will affect both the stability of the economy in which we work and future pension and insurance outcomes. Second, the wall of money was and is invested in any asset capable of generating future streams of income or capital gains, including commodities like grain, energy and metals – all essential to our daily lives and the green transition. Those in search of quick and easy capital gains chase any asset that can transfer income from the real sector to the finance sector.

What characterises these sought-after assets (property, commodities, works of art) is that all are *finite* in their supply, unlike the apparently limitless supply of money (credit) created by banks and by the world's savings poured into the shadow banking sector.

'Where will private equity aim its $9 trillion money hose?' asked the *Financial Times* in July 2024.

Private equity capital firms [are] sitting on an ungodly amount of capital after mammoth fundraising in 2020–21 and little investment in subsequent years . . . Morgan Stanley analysts reckon the pile of proverbial dry powder has now grown to about $4.5 tn – which, with leverage, means they are sitting on about $9 tn of buying power – and that this will need to be actually invested soon.[31]

Note the concern about the 'ungodly amount of capital' going nowhere. To maintain its value, the capital must be invested in income-generating assets. Yet it is precisely those assets that are finite in supply, security and availability. They include limited supplies of land (property) in its broadest sense and commodities (food, energy and metals). There are also limits to the supply of other more exotic assets, including historic works of art.

A wall of money invested in finite quantities of assets must inevitably inflate prices. And if the 'hose' of capital is switched off, prices must necessarily deflate. Therein lies a dilemma for managers of the world's savings. If pension and life insurance claims are to be honoured in the future, then they must be invested in assets that generate sufficient future income. Left in the bank as cash, even vast sums would earn little. Worse, the value of such vast sums of cash may fall, eroded by inflation. (Alternatively, and in a deflationary environment, when the general level of prices falls, the value of cash may increase.)

As noted earlier, fund managers can of course protect our pensions by investing in 'safe assets' like the debt (bonds) of sovereign countries like the United States and Britain. But those investments generate lower returns (interest) precisely because they are assumed to be safe. Furthermore, governments wedded to the ideology of austerity deliberately shrink the supply of debt (bonds). Investment or speculation in riskier assets – such as property or commodities – generate much higher rates of return than investment in sovereign bonds.

Which brings us back to the point of this chapter. Where do private managers invest this wall of money that includes our pension savings? We don't know whether our pensions are supporting the globalised property markets of London, Shanghai, Accra, Hanoi, New York, Rio de Janeiro or Berlin, or global infrastructure – working for the creation and use of clean energy and the restoration of nature's depleted resources. The money could be invested in wilfully obscure works of art, sold in a market described by one author as 'a celebration of capitalism at its most secretive and unregulated' and then stored in temperature-controlled vaults in tax avoidance domains like Dubai.[32] Or are our nest eggs invested in global commodity markets essential to humanity's survival – markets in food, energy and metals?

And what will be the impact of that wall of money on our living standards – and our future pension payments?

4

Speculation and Our Daily Bread

It's too much to expect the people who run big Wall Street firms to speak plain English, since so much of their livelihood depends on people believing that what they do cannot be translated into plain English.

Michael Lewis, *The Big Short*

If some of us grow rich in our sleep, where do we think this wealth is coming from? It doesn't materialise out of thin air. It doesn't come without costing someone, another human being. It comes from the fruits of others' labours, which they don't receive.

John Stuart Mill, *Principles of Political Economy*

Speculative Merry-Go-Rounds and the Hunger Profiteers

Back in 1721, the British artist William Hogarth illustrated the aftermath of a financial crisis known as the South Sea Bubble with a famous etching and engraving that satirised the greed that had led to the Bubble and subsequent crash.[1]

In the year before, thousands of investors and brokers across

Europe had embarked on a feverish bout of financial speculation in which vast sums of money were invested in fraudulent,
nonexistent and highly risky trading ventures. 'Both the rich
and the less affluent were falling under the thrall of the alluring
but fickle figure of Fortune', wrote one commentator. In Hogarth's print, the grossly mutilated figure of Fortune is shown
blindfolded,

> her body hacked by a scythe-wielding devil, who throws hunks
> of her flesh to the crazed speculators below. Honesty and Honour
> are similarly unclothed and exposed. Self-Interest is scourged by
> the two-faced figure of Villainy. Meanwhile, the frantic whirl of
> speculation is allegorised by the merry-go-round that spins in the
> mid-distance . . . Another form of gambling is highlighted on a
> nearby balcony, where a procession of spinsters queue to take
> part in a raffle for lottery-winning husbands.[2]

Hogarth did not pull his artistic punches.

There is nothing new about speculation. For centuries people
have gambled on future outcomes. For most of that time the
most honourable purpose of speculation was 'hedging' – a form
of insurance undertaken by responsible adults to deal with the
uncertainty of the future. Taking out insurance on one's home or
a car is a sensible form of hedging: protection from future losses
of an asset in which one has a direct interest. The insurance contract is a *derivative* because its premium payments are derived
from the underlying asset – the value of the property and the
associated risk to the insurer.

Throughout past centuries, judges, courts and the law have
recognised that there is a difference between hedging that serves
a social purpose and hedging that is mere speculation. Unlike
hedging that reduces risk, speculation increases risk and leads

to asset price bubbles, price volatility, manipulation schemes, reduced returns – and to inflation.

Hedge funds engage largely in speculation, not hedging. Which is why their title is a misnomer, perhaps a deliberate one. The owners and traders inside the fund are not hedging against risk. They are 'speculation funds', as their owners and traders use investment in futures, options and other derivative products to make quick profits by predicting short-term price changes at the expense of other traders. In a famous paper, Sanford Grossman and Joseph Stiglitz described speculators as 'careful researchers who invest in information that allows them to trade on superior terms with less-informed actors trading for consumption or other nonspeculative reasons'.[3] Speculation is the attempt to profit not from producing something, or even from providing investment funds to someone else who is producing something, but from predicting the future better than others predict it and then profiting from it.[4]

That is how most people regard speculation. However, mainstream economists take a different approach. Lynn A. Stout, a law professor explains, 'where popular opinion has long condemned speculation as a socially wasteful practice that distorts market prices, economic theory applauds speculation as promoting the economic goal of allocative efficiency.'[5] However, while most economists regard speculation as aiding efficiency, others regard the trade in speculative derivatives as improper because it is a form of rent-seeking: the attempt to acquire wealth not by creating it, but by effortlessly taking existing wealth from another.

Today, a speculator might try to make money by predicting the impact of a future event, say, wildfires in the Valencia region of Spain where the country's main citrus crops are grown. Because avocados are also grown in Valencia, speculators might bet on the likely failure of a crop and the consequent rise in the price of avocados.

Speculating in real (physical, or 'spot') markets for grains, property, gold or oil requires an investor to go to the actual expense of buying and holding stocks of grain, property, gold or oil. This is expensive and difficult because it involves significant capital outlays. Speculating through derivatives in global markets is much cheaper and easier and can be immensely more profitable.

Speculation and food price crises

The most essential commodities for our survival are wheat, soybeans and rice grains. These agricultural products are now instruments of financial speculation. Speculation in global grain markets inflates and deflates prices. By inflating prices, sustained speculation can trigger hunger on a worldwide scale.

Like other sectors in this book, the global agricultural industry operates well away from society's scrutiny. It is an immensely lucrative and secretive sector for those who are able to control major parts of it. The industry, known as the agri-commodity sector, is dominated by an oligopoly of four giant private multinationals that, through mergers and takeovers, control almost every stage of the supply chain of basic agricultural products such as cereals and oilseeds. The oligopoly enjoys superior bargaining power over farmers and other producers and faces little competition, except perhaps from the rise of the Chinese company COFCO International.

Together the Big Four agri-commodity companies control the world's grain stocks. They enforce harsh working conditions on employees in the agricultural and other sectors and accelerate environmental degradation, without society's constraints. None of the top four – Archer Daniels Midland (ADM), Bunge, Cargill and Louis Dreyfus Company (LDC) – is fully transparent in the disclosure of its trade volumes, and so it is difficult to verify information on them.[6] Nevertheless, in a 2024 report to the European Parliament, experts calculated that together they accounted for 50 to 60 per cent of the world trade in essential cereals, oilseed and protein crops in 2022.[7] It should come as no surprise that despite difficult trading conditions these past few years, the companies have reported extraordinary profits, especially in times of crises and high prices. Cargill reported profits of $117 billion in 2023, ADM $93 billion, Bunge $61 billion and LDC $59.9 billion.

The very fact that this oligopolistic structure (which could be considered an informal cartel) exists at all is unknown to the many millions who suffer from the impact of these companies on their daily lives. This should not surprise: our system of Western capitalism pivots public attention away from those who effectively govern markets and economies in the global sphere. The focus of national and European competition policies and institutions is on the domestic impact of consolidation and dominance through mergers and acquisitions in home markets. Consolidation and dominance in global markets are beyond their purview.

As a result, no government anywhere in the world has designated institutions, policies or rules to govern mergers and takeovers in the international sphere. Thanks to the Clinton administration's deregulation of global commodity markets (discussed later in this chapter), Western politicians oblige the owners of these hugely profitable and oligopolistic food corporations by turning a blind eye to their activities in financial markets. Nor is much attention paid to the broader public interest or to the environmental consequences of anti-competitive behaviour and abuse of market power by such companies. That neglect must bring considerable relief and satisfaction to executives, shareholders and family owners who make spectacular financial gains from the absence of competition, the lack of regulatory oversight and the steady expansion of their oligopolistic companies.

The combined speculative impact of this oligopoly and of financial speculators on food prices is what concerns us here. Food shocks are as devastating – economically as well as politically – as financial shocks, even while they attract far less attention. In 2025, the world was still in the grip of the cost-of-living crisis, but most commentators, including economists, were confused about its causes. Just as in 2008 when economists explained to the Queen of England that the Global Financial Crisis was both unforeseeable and inexplicable.

Beyond Supply and Demand

Spikes in grain prices are often explained by the economic theory of supply and demand for agricultural crops (including cocoa and coffee, now highly priced). I and many others contest that over-simplified explanation.[8] Rather, since President Clinton's deregulation of commodity markets in 2000, the majority of commodity traders on financial markets where prices are set are not real traders in the commodity, but financial players with little interest in investing in the agricultural sector. Instead they are keen to see higher prices for 'paper trades' on financial markets (derivatives contracts), which they can buy and sell at a profit without having agricultural products delivered to their door.

Demand and supply are the two main pillars of microeconomic theory. The theory is so powerful, it is often treated as a law. According to mainstream economics, 'supply and demand curves determine the price and quantity of goods and services. Any changes in supply and demand will have an effect on the equilibrium price and quantity of the good sold.'[9] Money and finance seldom enter into this picture of how prices are set in markets.

Instead, many economists and economic commentators incorrectly assume that commodity prices for grain and energy are solely determined by 'market forces'. At the national level, there is a public misperception that prices are determined in markets based on the home economy. These misperceptions are shared (or appear to be shared) by powerful politicians. When prices are high and supply scarce, politicians, persuaded by economic dogma that prices should *only* be set by market mechanisms, are reluctant to argue for interference in said markets.

Most economists, politicians and political commentators, when discussing price inflation, tend to ignore the role of finance and speculation in raising or lowering (agricultural and energy) prices. The focus invariably is on the labour force, with wages or supply chain disruptions and bad harvests blamed as a major cause of inflation.

It is undoubtedly the case that supply and demand, climate breakdown leading to bad harvests, geopolitical crises and wages all play a role in determining prices, but they are not the whole story. The impact of pricing and agri-business strategies in aggravating climate change and biodiversity loss is seldom, if ever, taken into account, even while the climate crisis wreaks havoc on food production and harvests. The additional force at play is the global system of financial speculation: betting or gambling in the Global Casino on whether the price of an asset like wheat, corn or soybeans will rise or fall.

Speculation as well as supply and demand shocks can lead to both a rise in prices in futures markets and volatility in food prices. Many argue that because volatility in markets can be immensely profitable to speculators, volatility encourages speculation in both agricultural and energy markets.

Two types of traders exist in agricultural markets. The first is big farmers and commercial (real) traders, whose main business is in growing, buying and selling commodities. They hedge against price swings, but also speculate on price movements. On the other hand, there are the 'paper' gamblers. The latter, unlike the former, do not hold stocks of the commodity. They simply place bets on the likely rise or fall in a commodity's price. A few also trade for small farmers who cannot trade on derivatives markets themselves.

Agricultural derivatives (assets that are financial contracts) can be traded on a commodity exchange or outside an exchange, between two individuals or institutions, betting 'over the counter' (OTC) that a derivative will rise or fall in price. As Professor Stout explains, calling this form of trading 'over the counter' obscures the nature of the activity: betting on the horses.[10] The arcane language is designed to confuse and hide what is really going on.

Speculative traders on exchanges influence and increase or lower volatility and price hikes. OTC trading is opaque, making it hard to track trades by speculators. Those include hedge fund managers, pension fund investors, swap dealers, high frequency traders, investment bankers and the managers of exchange-traded funds (ETFs).

Their speculation costs lives. It also fosters greed and corruption of individuals, institutions and societies. It undermines the values of decency and transparency. It is extractive of the ecosystem's precious and finite resources and it is exploitative of labour. Above all, it can lead, as it did in 2007–9, to food riots due to high prices and, as on many occasions before, can contribute to a global cataclysmic breakdown of the economy.

The 2005–8 Hunger Games

Remember the hunger of 2005–8? Probably not. In the run-up to the Global Financial Crisis, there was the global food price crisis. It was a crisis for hungry people living in the poorest countries of the world. Over three years, global food prices rose by a whopping 83 per cent as speculation in financial markets accelerated. Between January 2005 and June 2008, maize prices almost tripled, wheat prices increased 127 per cent and rice prices increased 170 per cent. Higher prices pushed an additional 40 million people into hunger in 2008, raising the overall number of undernourished people in the world to 963 million, compared to 923 million in 2007.[11]

According to the economist Anuradha Mittal, the greater demand created by investors' activities in commodity futures markets (where hedging and speculation are both allowed) put tremendous upward price pressure on food and energy commodities. The higher prices applied to essential foodstuffs, including corn, rice and soya. Wheat, a commodity increasingly subject to speculative trade in commodity futures exchanges, was subject to extreme price volatility. Prices rose by 46 per cent between January and February 2008 but fell by as much by May that year.[12] These prices were correlated with the greater participation of hedge funds, index funds and sovereign wealth funds in agricultural commodity markets – especially after 2006.

The food price rises of 2005–8 led to riots in many countries. A 2009 report from the UN's Food and Agriculture Organization (FAO) estimated that the number of people going hungry every day had reached a historic high at 1.02 billion people, one-sixth of humanity.[13] According to the FAO, as of April 2008, corn volatility was 30 per cent and soybean volatility 40 per cent beyond what could be accounted for by market fundamentals.[14]

Michael Masters is the founder and chair of the non-profit organisation Better Markets and a global expert on the subject of speculation in commodities markets. Prices of food spiked, he told a US Senate committee, because speculators were buying up essential commodities with the sole purpose of 'reaping speculative profits'.[15]

But what is striking about the 2005–8 food shock is this fact: more food had been produced by 2008 than at any point in human history. At the same time, demand for food was falling as the global economy weakened and then collapsed from August 2007 onwards.[16]

The economic law of supply and demand, so often called upon as explanation of the cause of such crises, did not apply here. Instead, the price volatility that led to hunger and food riots was caused by the greater participation of financial speculators in food derivatives markets. That in turn was a direct result of the Clinton administration's 2000 change to the Roosevelt administration's 1936 Commodity Exchange Act, changes which removed quantitative restrictions on speculative positions in agricultural futures contracts.

The 2022–5 Global Cost-of-Living Crisis

In 2022, Russia invaded Ukraine, and once again the world suffered a global food shock. By early 2025, the world was still in the throes of a cost-of-living crisis caused by high energy, food and land (property) prices. Over three years, the UK consumer price index jumped by 21.6 per cent.[17] Insecure middle-class individuals and families across the world were choosing between heating and eating, and the low-paid, job-insecure poorest were going hungry. Some were starving. The food shock of 2022 – when global food and energy prices surged – caused 71 million people in low-income countries to fall into poverty in just three months.[18] According to the UN, the impact on poverty rates was drastically faster than the shock of the COVID-19 pandemic.

In Britain, the Resolution Foundation explained that while energy prices rose faster, food made up a far larger share of the typical household's consumption (13 per cent versus 5 per cent in 2019–20). Food price inflation reached around 19 per cent in March 2023, the highest in almost fifty years. By the summer of 2023, the food price shock threatened to overtake the energy price shock as the biggest threat to family finances.[19]

In 2018, according to Dr Megan Blake of Sheffield University, about 10 per cent of the British adult population were skipping meals or going without food. By the middle of 2020, the rate was 16 per cent. In the autumn of 2022, the rate was 24 per cent. In 2022, those who struggled most were adults living in the most deprived communities (40 per cent), those on incomes less than £32,000 per year (46 per cent) and those who were not employed (45 per cent). By 2022, one in four British working adults were also food insecure, up from 16 per cent in 2020.[20] Those worrying facts are about people living in one of the richest countries in the world. At the same time, between January 2020 and March 2022, thanks to capital mobility, investment funds were able to increase their commodity net buying positions by almost four times, according to data from Euronext, Europe's leading commodity exchange.[21]

People suffering the cost-of-living crisis may not have followed the arcane activities of investors on exchanges in remote global commodity markets, but many understood that at root, the rise in food prices was a consequence of globalisation and 'big economic interests'. For instance, at the World Trade Organization (WTO), low-income nations were not allowed to hold food stocks because the US was able to block such reserves to protect

US farmers and its agribusiness (three of the four dominant players are US headquartered) exports. Leaders of low-income countries also understood the crisis as an injustice inflicted on the working classes. Food security has not been part of the WTO's remit, nor has the international institution countered the growth of globalised corporate concentration as a consequence of its rules.

Public anger was widespread. Blame fell on centrist politicians like President von der Leyen of the European Commission, President Ramaphosa of South Africa, Prime Minister Modi of India and most catastrophically on US President Biden, whose Democratic Party was heavily defeated in the 2024 elections. Inflation and the combined volatility of energy, food and property market prices were key factors that led voters to focus on far-right politicians like Donald Trump, Marine Le Pen and Victor Orbán.

Populist leaders promised 'protection' from globalisation. Victor Orbán called for Hungarian economic independence in the face of popular frustration with 'the unfavourable consequences of globalisation'.[22] The leader of France's far-right National Rally party, Marine Le Pen, in a debate with Emmanuel Macron in May 2017, accused her opponent in the presidential race of being 'the candidate of unbridled globalisation, of Uberisation, of hardship, of social brutality, of the war of all against all, of the economic ransacking of our big groups, of the dismemberment of France by the big economic interests'.[23]

How Clinton's Changes to the Law Triggered Food Crises

Lynn A. Stout, an American professor of law, argues that flawed economic reasoning about the cause of these crises arises among economists *because* they are economists, not lawyers. The credit crisis, she writes, 'was not due primarily to changes in the markets, it was due to changes in the law'.[24] Following her reasoning leads to an examination of the most significant recent change to commodity market law, authorised by President Clinton in 2000 and devised by Alan Greenspan (chair of the Federal Reserve) and Lawrence Summers (secretary of the US Treasury).

While the Clinton administration's decision to weaken and repeal the 1933 Banking Act (Glass–Steagall) is well known, far less known are the changes made to the 1936 Commodity Exchange Act. Those changes were embodied in the Clinton-era statute, the Commodities Futures Modernization Act of 2000 (CFMA). This 'modernisation' of law related to commodity trading would precipitate food crises, as well as economic and political crises, in both 2005–8 and again in 2022–4.

Professor Larry Summers (at the time President Clinton's Treasury secretary) and Chairman Alan Greenspan, encouraged by Wall Street lobbying, had persuaded President Clinton and lawmakers that further financialisation of the commodities market might make the market more 'efficient' by promoting 'innovation, competition, efficiency, liquidity, and transparency in over-the-counter derivatives markets, by providing legal certainty for OTC derivatives and removing impediments to innovation (specifically to the development of electronic trading systems)'.[25]

The 'working group' wanted to exclude opaque OTC derivative trading from the legal constraints embodied in the 1936 Commodity Exchange Act. They supported 'bilateral transactions between sophisticated (sic) counterparties' and 'electronic trading systems'. After the 2000 Commodity Modernisation Act was passed, speculative trading in commodities vital to the welfare of human society became subject to a volatile arms race that amplified or inflated and deflated prices as markets swung wildly up or down.

Financial instruments or securities – let's call them poker chips – that are the subject of speculative trading are largely detached from the value of the underlying asset. The asset (agricultural commodity) appears irrelevant to the speculator. Prices set by the poker chips, or OTC derivatives, are driven by the same magical thinking that informed the booming property market prior to the Global Financial Crisis. This thinking is accelerated by a herd mentality and by ever-escalating competition between speculators. It laid the ground for the hungry years of 2005–8 and the cost-of-living crisis of 2022–4.

Before the Clinton Act was passed in 2000, Professor Stout had warned of the dangers posed by proposals for a sudden and wholesale removal of centuries-old legal constraints on speculative trading in OTC derivatives. In a paper published in 1995 titled 'Betting the Bank: How Derivatives Trading Under Conditions of Uncertainty Can Increase Risks and Erode Returns in Financial Markets', Professor Stout warned of the threat posed by derivatives to society as a whole:

> Academics and policymakers alike have praised financial derivatives as archetypes of financial progress and innovation. As the victim list grows longer, however, the notion that the burgeoning derivatives markets offer unmixed blessings seems increasingly implausible. Trading in these volatile instruments clearly can be hazardous to the health of the corporations, banks, municipalities and pension and mutual funds that indulge in it. As the body count rises, it becomes difficult not to suspect that derivatives trading may also impose significant costs on society as a whole.
>
> Federal regulators concerned about the potential downsides to derivatives have focused on the possibility that *derivatives trading contributes to 'systemic risk,'* meaning that a derivatives-induced failure of one of the large financial institutions involved

in this concentrated market could trigger a chain of related firm failures, including failures of federally insured banks.[26]

Her warnings were ignored. As were the warnings issued by Brooksley Born, then chair of the Commodity Futures Trading Commission (CFTC), the federal agency that oversees the US futures and commodity options markets. In October 1998, Ms Born warned in congressional testimony that the dangerous boom in OTC derivatives trading could 'threaten our regulated markets or, indeed, our economy without any federal agency knowing about it'.[27]

In a television interview that aired in 2009, well after the law had changed, Ms Born explained that the Clinton Commodity Modernisation Act of 2000

> took away all jurisdiction of over-the-counter derivatives from the CFTC. It also took away any potential jurisdiction . . . on the part of the Securities Exchange Commission, and in fact, forbid state regulators from interfering with the over-the-counter derivatives markets. In other words, it exempted it from all government oversight, all oversight on behalf of the public interest. [28]

The warnings of both Professor Stout and Ms Born were summarily dismissed by President Clinton's powerful Working Group on Financial Markets, headed up by Alan Greenspan and US Treasury Secretary Lawrence Summers. They jointly signed a report to the president in November 1999 and spelt out the changes they believed were needed to deregulate OTC derivatives markets. Their report gushed with enthusiasm for the role OTC derivatives had played in commodity markets, a role they believed would be enhanced with further deregulation:

'Over-the-counter derivatives have transformed the world of finance increasing the range of financial products available to corporations and investors and fostering more precise ways of understanding, quantifying, and managing risk. These important markets are large and growing rapidly.'[29]

The report was right about one thing: the 'wall of money' involved in OTC derivatives speculation. 'At the end of 1998, the estimated notional value of OTC derivative contracts was $80 trillion, according to the Bank for International Settlements.'[30]

The Chicago Mercantile Exchange (CME)

Most speculation on the future prices of wheat, corn and soybeans takes place in a global market based in Chicago – the Chicago Mercantile Exchange (CME). Producers, traders and speculators 'manage risk and capture opportunities' by laying bets on 'futures and options' in foodstuffs at the CME, not in markets based in London, Johannesburg or Rio de Janeiro. The CME is a giant global marketplace where prices for vital commodities are ultimately fixed. For each commodity essential to human well-being and to the green transition, including grains, the most important market for trading and pricing is the CME. The CME therefore sets global price benchmarks.

A wall of speculative money aimed at Chicago's global market in grain has a systemically important and global impact: inflation in the prices of those commodities. Other impacts include collapse of prices in the event of a sudden and excessive change in confidence (Keynes's 'animal spirits') or of changes in other financial markets deemed more profitable.

According to an analysis by Société Générale, the speculative strategies by a group of ten hedge funds active on the CME were able to make a profit of $1.9 billion based on the price spike of wheat, maize and soybeans following the start of the war in Ukraine.[31] The volatility of commodity prices set at the Chicago Mercantile Exchange has major impacts on the world's consumers of grains, especially those in the poorest countries. When a wall of speculative money is aimed at limited supplies of an asset like grain, prices rocket upwards.

What Must Be Done?

To restore stability to the prices of society's most important commodities, we must comprehensively transform the international financial architecture – a grand ambition, but in the event of another global crisis, a necessary one.

What to do in the meantime? Professor Stout thinks the answer is obvious: go back to what worked well, for so long, before. 'The old common law rule against difference contracts was a simple, elegant legal sieve that separated useful hedging contracts from purely speculative wagers.'[32]

It did so by protecting 'useful hedging contracts' and *declining to enforce* 'hedging contracts from purely speculative wagers'. As she notes in her Lombard Street paper, there is no cheaper form of government intervention than inaction, for the state to use the power of the law to refuse to enforce a deal or contract. In other words, the law could not be used to enforce the terms of an over-the-counter contract if it were broken. That would bring speculators down to earth and force them to be much more careful before making bets that could not be honoured by reference to the law.[33]

Additional steps could be taken to deal with commodity price speculation, as a group of economists led by the economist Professor Weber have demonstrated.[34] The first step would be to 'follow the money'. That requires the United States and other

OECD countries to set stricter position limits for financial companies that are active on commodity futures markets. In other words, large traders and financial institutions would be constrained – as they were before the year 2000 – in the number of shares or derivative contracts ('poker chips') a trader or group of traders may own and use to corner the market.

In the meantime, there is a need for governments – especially governments of low-income countries – to build up buffer stocks of key staple foods such as maize, rice, wheat, vegetable oils and other products at strategically important locations. Unfortunately, World Trade Organization (WTO) rules restrict rights for public food stockholding, precisely to leave price setting of exports to global financial markets and big traders. In February 2024, a group of thirty-three low-income nations tried to obtain a permanent solution to greater stockholding flexibility, but they were defeated by WTO decision-making rules.[35]

Yet stock building need not be a utopian daydream, as the economist Isabella Weber and her colleagues argue in their proposal for a scheme for public food stocks that would stabilise prices and transform food systems.[36] China and India, the world's two most populous countries, have for years been operating public food storage facilities.[37] But the most well known of the world's buffer stocks is held by the United States of America at the Department of Energy. The Strategic Petroleum Reserve (SPR) is an emergency reserve for offsetting oil supply shortages and stabilising prices set on speculative global markets – a reserve which President Biden used. Another solution would be fixing the total amount of speculative trading positions allowed in a particular market, while still allowing enough hedging counterparties. However, these solutions would operate within the current system whereby prices are set on derivatives markets, without consideration of production and consumer prices. There is still the danger that climate change will result in sky-high prices if harvests fail. The challenge is how to guarantee prices that would allow farmers to move to more climate-resilient and rural-friendly production, while also ensuring affordable consumer prices and avoiding excessive profits throughout the chain. Markets have failed to do so, and politicians have no understanding or political will to explore other price-setting systems, either domestically and internationally, beyond the simplistic law of supply and demand as applied to physical and financial or derivatives markets.

If governments chose to manage public buffer stocks of essential grains, international coordination would be necessary for managing the system. The long-neglected United Nations Food and Agriculture Organization (FAO) would be well suited to that purpose. Finally, governments need to mandate stricter transparency for food trading companies, with a view to limiting the information leverage held by the five largest agricultural trading companies.

In other words, action and even inaction by governments could quickly put a stop to the frenzied activities of speculators in global commodity markets. All it takes is wider public understanding of the issues and the mobilisation of political will.

5

Playing Poker with the Energy System

Speculators in the Global Casino help inflate or deflate prices for commodities like energy and other assets. By aiming a 'fire hose' of finance at these finite assets, they help increase prices. By withdrawing the fire hose, they deflate prices. In 2025, both the commercial banking sector and the shadow banking sector held or managed about $417 trillion in liquid deposits – 'financial assets'.[1] Global GDP – income derived from real economic activity – amounts to just $105 trillion. Holders of the world's excess savings – about $300 trillion – are always on the lookout for assets that will generate 'rent', or interest on those savings.

Energy, like food and grains, is one of the most desirable of those assets. Oil, gas, diesel, coal, wind and solar play major roles in supplying energy to the world's people – from those on the Shetland Islands in the north of Britain to those crowded in poor housing in Lagos, Nigeria, or in the bustling suburbs of Hanoi, Vietnam. But how and where are the prices of those immensely important commodities determined? The generally accepted view is that prices are set in domestic markets, according to the laws of 'supply and demand'. National and regional markets for energy commodities are complex and varied across continents, but ultimately prices – especially for oil and gas – are determined in global commodity markets. The most important of these are the Chicago Mercantile Exchange in the US and Euronext N.V. for Europe. And while real trades between suppliers and buyers of oil, gas and other forms of energy are important, speculators in the Global Casino play a major, if hidden, role too.

The price of crude oil rose from around $40 per barrel in the second half of 2020 to a peak of $115 in June 2022 triggering a global cost-of-living crisis. Oil prices are systemically important to economies because energy is a critical input into the production of most goods and services and is therefore vital to prices and price stability overall.[2]

The Rocketing Cost of Energy

'We pay the highest energy bills in the country', a woman declared, startling the audience in the Mareel Arts Centre on Scotland's Shetland Island. The anger in her voice was vehement and was echoed by others. It was a glorious day in the spring of 2024, and I was visiting the remote island, the most northerly archipelago of the United Kingdom, as a member of the Scottish government's Just Transition Commission. Inside the Arts Centre in Lerwick, the island's capital, we were taking evidence from local community leaders.

The island is one of the windiest places in Britain. It already has ample offshore and onshore wind energy, but expects soon to host the country's biggest-ever onshore wind farm of 103 giant turbines: SSE's Viking project. Shetland has also pioneered tidal energy. It has three 100 kW turbines that make up the first offshore tidal array in the world to deliver electricity to homes and businesses on the island.[3]

Given this abundance of local clean energy supplies, why were Shetlanders paying the highest bills in the country? The answer is that despite all that clean energy, the main generators of the island's energy supply are oil, diesel and gas (with both diesel and gas derived from crude oil). Electricity is piped into the homes of Shetlanders by the diesel-fired Lerwick Power Station, a heavy fuel oil, light gas oil generator that has provided reliable power to islanders since 1953.[4] The low cost of wind energy does not play any part in fixing the cost of Shetland's energy bills. Britain has privatised markets in energy and electricity, where prices are determined in 'wholesale' energy markets operating in the Global Casino.

Energy prices are high because islanders use unregulated, imported fuels for heating. Add to that the fact that many Shetland homes have poor insulation, and many households don't have access to mains gas. Tough for a climate that is windy and cold. That helps explain why Shetland's estimated household energy bills are nearly double the average UK figure.

Three kinds of participants in energy markets serve Shetland. First, generators who create and sell the real stuff, the power – coal, nuclear, oil, wind and solar. The second group are electricity suppliers who buy energy for resale to consumers. The third group are speculators.

The energy market resembles a tower

Britain's energy market, like many others, has a range of suppliers. Arranged like a tower, suppliers constitute a hierarchy of providers, with coal and nuclear at the base and gas at the top. Coal and nuclear sectors generate 'baseload' supplies, meaning that supply is continuous and not easily switched on or off. Oil and gas generators are more flexible, while wind and solar are intermittent.

In short, while reliable baseload suppliers are important, so too are energy suppliers that step up and meet peak demand – when the nation takes a break, say, from a World Cup match and switches on millions of kettles.

Natural gas – a fossil fuel – is at the top of the hierarchy, the most reliable 'peak' supplier of energy, but is also the most expensive. Each additional unit of energy costs gas suppliers more than it does other energy suppliers. Marginal costs are effectively zero for the wind and solar suppliers, because there are no fuel costs. If wind and power generators were setting energy prices, they would effectively be fixed at zero.

But that is not how the current market-based system works on the island of Shetland, or indeed anywhere else in Britain. The peak supplier and most expensive generator of energy, the gas sector, sets the price delivered by all generators. Why? The reasoning behind it, according to the *Economist*, is that 'just like any other market for a homogeneous good, the price of power is set by the most expensive supplier'.[5] In other words, generators are all supplying the same thing, energy, so they should all be paid the same.

As a result, the input and carbon costs of generating natural gas helps determine the wholesale market price for all generators. The British Institute for Government explains it this way:

> Although generation methods that have low marginal cost (including renewables and nuclear) produce the majority of UK electricity, the price that is paid for it in both wholesale and retail markets is set much higher, at the marginal cost of generating electricity with gas. That price is in turn influenced by speculators in the global market for gas.[6]

The net result of all this is that because Shetland is so dependent on fossil fuels, because the price of generating energy is set by the most expensive energy provider – gas – energy bills on the island are high. Gas sets the UK's wholesale price of electricity for a more significant proportion of the time than in other European countries.

Windfalls for wind farms

When the Scottish Just Transition Commission visited the Isle of Lewis in the Outer Hebrides in late 2023, we learned that the local community-owned wind farm (and indeed all the surrounding commercial wind farms) had enjoyed a literal windfall from the spike in energy prices between 2021 and much of 2022. That was because the marginal cost of pricing meant that all energy generators benefited, not just the gas sector. The biggest beneficiaries were generators with low operating costs – the wind and solar generators.

At a Stornoway town hall meeting with Commission members, angry businessmen and women expressed hostility to the towering wind turbines viewed from their gardens. They complained of little benefit from locally generated clean energy. The reason for their discontent was that renewable energy generators charge retail customers the global, volatile market-based price that is a feature of fossil fuel energy generation – not the local, cost-related price of generating clean wind energy. And because all UK-based energy generated locally is exported via the national grid and distributed across the country to be shared with Europe, those living near wind farms do not benefit from the towering structures that pepper their countryside.

The structure of the market, however, is good for the fossil fuel sector, which made massive profits over the years of the COVID pandemic and when Russia blocked the supply of natural gas to

Europe after 2021.[7] Centrica, which owns British Gas, made
£758 million from its electricity generation business in 2022, of
which £753 million was for nuclear generation.[8] Over the same
period typical household energy bills on the Isle of Lewis and
elsewhere had increased by 54 per cent in April 2022 and by 27
per cent in October 2022.[9]

Where Is the Market for Energy Based?

In the US, gas is traded on spot basis based on the Henry Hub
gas hub. In Europe, it is traded mainly using the virtual gas hubs
such as the National Balancing Point in the UK and Title Transfer Facility (TTF) in the Netherlands, which is the main
European hub, allocating over two-thirds of all relevant trades.[10]

The TTF virtual market brings together both national and
international energy producers, storage companies, distributors
and network operators. It is where traders buy and sell gas supplies and, in the process, determine the price.

But how is the price of gas fixed? As with all major commodities, in globalised markets and by global market forces. Those
include three markets for fixing the price of gas. First, the physical market for gas (the spot market). Second, the 'paper markets'
for gas, such as the New York Mercantile Exchange and the
Chicago Mercantile Exchange (CME). Third, the retail market
for gas (the street price).

IG is a global trading platform for trading and speculating in
natural gas. Its website helpfully explains how to engage in the
paper markets to speculate on natural gas prices. The first strategy involves 'futures contracts'.

The most common way that traders take a position on natural
gas with a futures contract, such as the Henry Hub natural gas

futures contract on the Chicago Mercantile Exchange. With a futures contract, traders agree to the delivery of a certain amount of natural gas at a set date in the future for an agreed-upon price. However, this means that the trader may have to eventually take delivery of the asset.

With IG, you can speculate on the price of a futures contract – without taking ownership of the underlying asset – with a CFD or contracts for difference. (CFD trading is the buying and selling of contracts for difference – which are financial derivatives that let you take a speculative position on whether an asset [including shares, indices, cryptos, commodities and forex] will rise or fall in value.)

Aside from futures, traders can use options to speculate on the price of natural gas. There are two types of options, puts and calls, both of which give traders the right but not the obligation to buy or sell an underlying asset before a certain expiry date.[11]

Energy consumers and bill payers in Shetland and the rest of the UK are exposed to global market forces and volatility in prices traded on platforms like IG and in markets in which trading, hedging and speculation push prices up and down. That volatility affects prices across the spectrum of energy generators. Low-cost renewable energy benefits, but also loses, from the rise and fall in prices as much as does the natural gas industry.

The Globalised Oil Market

Citing the high price of oil, Senator Joe Manchin killed off one of President Biden's legislative efforts to tackle climate change: the Build Back Better Act. He did so by framing the problem of oil price inflation in terms of supply: 'How do we bring down the price of gasoline?' Answering his own question, he said, 'from the energy thing, but you can't do it *unless you produce more*. If there's people that don't want to produce more fossil, then you got a problem. That's just reality. You got to do it' (emphasis added).[12]

Does Senator Manchin really believe that increasing the supply of oil will bring down prices? The senator's blind spot for the role of global finance in fixing energy prices is common to most politicians – not just to Wall Street's friends.

The economists Carlotta Breman and Servaas Storm have set about trying to show just how influential speculators are in the market for 'black gold' – and how much that speculation impacted inflation in the US. As many economists accept, hedge fund managers and other speculators are active in the oil market, and their activity has raised the volume of oil transactions far above the volume warranted by ordinary commercial transactions.[13] The two economists focus on whether the sharp increases in prices from 2020 to 2022 were due to fundamental shifts in supply and demand or whether they must be attributed (at least partly) to excessive market speculation.

They concluded, according to their model analysis, that excessive speculation in the crude oil market was responsible for 24 to 48 per cent of the increase in the WTI (West Texas Intermediate) crude price from October 2020 to June 2022. These estimates translated into an oil price increase of around $18 to $36 per barrel and an increase in the US inflation rate of 0.75 to 1.5 percentage points during that same period.

While supply and demand have undoubtedly played a role in the dramatic volatility of oil, gas and food prices, the real cause of this instability (both the highs and their subsequent crashes) lies elsewhere. Understanding this matters because the astronomical rise in the oil price has had severe and, in some places, catastrophic consequences for the world's people. Add to that, the oil price shock has accelerated climate breakdown, because in order to substitute for costlier fossil fuels, countries (like Germany) fired up their coal mines.

Why it is wrong to blame Russia, Saudi Arabia or ExxonMobil
To understand how the global oil market works, it helps to compare the power of Russia, Saudi Arabia or ExxonMobil over the price of a barrel of oil to Tesla's power over the price of its electric vehicle. In 2025, Tesla's price was high, with the company charging a gross margin of about 30 per cent on each car sold. The ability to set that price and margin is exclusively determined by executives at Tesla, with demand for its cars of course playing a role.

For car manufacturers there is no global terminal market where speculators play a role in fixing the price of, for example, Tesla cars. That price can be adjusted by Tesla executives to changes in global demand and to changes in currency markets to ensure the gross margin holds wherever cars are sold. In contrast, while Russian dictators, Saudi princes and ExxonMobil or BP executives can influence the *supply* of oil, they do not have power over *the price* of a barrel of oil.

Vladimir Putin – whose words are never to be trusted – was right when he claimed (in June 2022) that Russia did not set oil prices. 'The market', he said, 'is raising energy prices, not Russia.'[14] Much of Putin's political power derives from the market's role in raising energy prices and filling his country's vaults with the proceeds. Researcher Yaneer Bar-Yam estimates that from 2002 to 2012, Russia received up to an additional $560 billion from financial speculators alone. Much of this windfall came directly from Wall Street and the City of London, writes the author and filmmaker Rupert Russell.[15] When oil prices were low, as in the 1990s, Russian dictators like President Yeltsin lacked the geopolitical power now wielded by President Putin.

In the more recent past the oil majors have experienced significant losses from the market's big price falls, as oil company defenders have argued.

> The past 10 years, major oil and gas companies suffered tremendous losses in 2014, 2015, and 2020. In fact, in 2020 the five integrated super-majors (i.e., 'Big Oil') – ExxonMobil, BP, Shell, Chevron, and Total – lost $76 billion. Oil prices plunged into negative territory in 2020.[16]

At the same time there has been a huge influx of speculative dollars in energy commodities, even while the ability of the Commodity Futures Trading Commission (CFTC) to monitor the nature, extent and effect of this speculation has been diminishing. Most significantly, there has been an explosion of trading of US energy commodities on exchanges that are not regulated by the CFTC.

Speculators are playing poker with the economy and ecosystem, and holding society to ransom in the process. This should concern us all. Why should management of the price of fuel, which threatens both our ecosystem and our economies, be beyond the reach and regulation of democratic (or even undemocratic) states and their citizens?

6

The Financialisation of Housing

At the heart of the cost-of-living crisis of 2021–4 was the house price inflation crisis. Unaffordable housing played a big part in the subsequent election of authoritarian governments, including that of Donald Trump to the American presidency in 2024. In the United States housing was, as David Dayen explains, 'one aspect of the Consumer Price Index that has refused to be tamed. The greatest swing toward Donald Trump in the presidential election came in urban centers like Chicago and New York City, where rising housing prices and homelessness are most acute.'[1]

Increasingly in advanced economies and also emerging markets, the distinction between the use value of land or property as a domestic or commercial residence and its market value as a financial asset that enables unearned capital gains (and rent extraction) is becoming blurred, as Ryan-Collins and colleagues argue.[2] As land and house prices rise faster than incomes over a lengthy period of time, the owners of wealth increasingly view property not just as a place to live but as a financial investment.

In advanced economies, banks' main activity is now domestic mortgage lending.[3] A recent study of credit in seventeen countries found that the share of mortgage loans in banks' total lending portfolios has roughly doubled over the course of the past century – from about 30 per cent in 1900 to about 60 per cent today.

Between 2011 and 2017, and as a result of the foreclosure crisis in which millions lost their homes, the US government provided incentives to Wall Street firms to buy up empty unsold houses.[4] These firms, including private equity groups and hedge funds, spent $36 billion acquiring more than 200,000 homes across the country. In one district, Atlanta, they bought almost 90 per cent of the 7,500 homes sold between January 2011 and June 2012. Today, institutional investors own at least one in five single-family rentals in some parts of the Atlanta metro area.[5]

In 2017, Blackstone, the private equity firm, was the 'largest landlord for single-family rentals in the world and the largest landlord' in the US.[6] In recent years, Wall Street financial conglomerates like the Blackstone Group have been buying up tens of thousands of houses across the country, making them a growing force in the residential rental housing industry.

The US was not an outlier. Housing costs around the world were rocketing, including in cities such as Accra, Ghana (where researchers conclude only the wealthy can own a home) and El Poblado in Medellín, Colombia.[7] In Ghana, the capital has undergone a major transformation: there are no restrictions on foreigners buying property. Ghana's real estate boom and 'housing deficit presents not just a challenge but also a golden opportunity for savvy investors'.[8] In Medellín, Colombia, a real estate guide reminds potential investors that 'Laureles, one of Medellin's prime neighbourhoods, recently earned the title of the coolest neighbourhood globally by *Time Out Global Magazine . . .*

Laureles now thrives as a hotspot for digital nomads, entrepreneurs, and investors, drawn by its perfect blend of tranquillity and opportunity.'[9]

Buying a home means taking on high levels of debt – a risk when incomes were not rising at the same pace. Human beings all need a safe, adequate roof over their heads. A place to call home is what makes life bearable and fulfilment possible. It is surely one of our fundamental human rights. But in many countries housing is not a right but a privilege. To be denied that right is to live in an uncivilised society. The Global Casino plays a big part in denying millions of people the right to decent, affordable housing. And in doing so, it is placing the global financial system at risk. As the Global Financial Crisis of 2007 demonstrated, banks in both the commercial and shadow banking sectors were exposed to the risk of falls in house prices, wherever they happened in the world. On this occasion, the gamble was a disaster for the Global Casino, but once again, the ones who felt it the most were homeowners and renters.

In Anglo-American countries housing serves two economic functions. On the one hand, it is a consumption good, providing shelter, proximity to work and a place to raise a family. On the other, it has been made into a financial asset for speculative investment, accumulation and extraction. However, today the balance has tipped towards housing as a commodity. Millions of the world's people are trapped in the grip of an economic system in which the right to a home is dispensed by the ruthless hand of the market, based largely on Wall Street.

Yet housing (land), like labour and money, is totally unsuited to the operation of the market. Neither land, labour nor money are commodities, and yet under capitalism all three are wrongly treated as if they are. As Karl Polanyi famously argued, under capitalist ideology, land became a commodity, albeit a 'fictional commodity'. Unlike commodities such as grains, metals or energy, land cannot be 'produced' by human labour and capital. Mark Twain is said to have advised, 'Buy land. They don't make it anymore.'

In economic terms, land is inelastic – a gift of nature and finite in its supply.[10] (The exception being Dubai's sandy artificial archipelago of islands. Palm Jumeirah is 'home to some of the most expensive properties in the world'.[11]) Land, unlike other commodities, cannot be reproduced or used up. Above all, land (and property) is confined by boundaries. It cannot be moved out of the United States, Ireland, New Zealand or Brazil.

The supply of credit, by contrast, is elastic, and with the help of both domestic monetary policy (the deregulation of credit creation and interest rate setting) and the activities of the Global Casino, credit can be produced almost ad infinitum by both global and domestic monetary and financial institutions. And unlike land, credit and capital are not confined by boundaries. In our globalised world, capital has been granted the immense and unaccountable power of frictionless mobility.

To understand a nation's housing crisis we must of course be cognisant of local conditions: increased demand as a result of the rise of migration from rural to urban areas, the rise (or falls) in local incomes, the rise of Airbnb and the impact of government policies. Then there is the creation of 'charter cities', new libertarian jurisdictions on empty land with their own legal frameworks and governance systems, especially in Africa. These places remove democratic oversight in the development of the city. In short, they are designed 'to separate political power from wealth'.[12] But even while assessing local conditions we must lift our eyes to the global macroeconomy. Real estate assets are highly localised, with revenue streams mostly contingent on regional dynamics, yet real estate capital markets are highly globalised. This is in part due to the presence of institutional capital such as mobile private equity firms, sovereign wealth and pension, hedge and insurance funds. All have global investment mandates, and all are keen to acquire assets against which they seek to leverage both future income and new debt.

We need to follow the great tide of money from the Global Casino that is aimed at national markets offering fixed supplies of real estate. A proportion of that finance (credit) is created and 'managed' by the private non-bank financial sector within the Global Casino. It is measured narrowly by the Financial Stability Board at $70 trillion. 'The narrow measure consists of Non-Bank Financial Intermediation entities ('shadow banks') involved in credit intermediation activities . . . could give rise to bank-like vulnerabilities because they involve liquidity/maturity transformation or use of leverage.'[13]

'Credit intermediation' here means credit creation. 'Maturity transformation' means borrowing short-term to lend long-term. For example, commercial banks might borrow short to lend a customer $300,000 to be repaid at a profitable interest over the long term. The process is risky and gives rise to 'vulnerabilities', such as those faced by the failed Northern Rock Bank, which borrowed on volatile international markets and then caused a run on the bank when investors got nervous that the bank had no money on their books.[14] According to the FSB, $70 trillion of global finance creation faces such 'bank-like vulnerabilities'. This $70 trillion has to be invested in assets that promise a good return. Property is one of those assets.

But $70 trillion is but one part of the $486.4 trillion of finance generated by both the regulated global banking system and the unregulated Global Casino.[15] Contrast that with the income generated by real economic activity. At the end of 2024, global GDP – the global income generated by 194 economies – was projected by the IMF to amount to just around \$110.06 trillion in nominal terms.[16] While the \$486 trillion from finance can largely be categorised as 'debt' or obligations (to provide future pensions or insurance obligations), it must ultimately be repaid out of income. Given that global income is just a quarter of global finance, there is a risk that some part of global debt repayments and other obligations may not be met.

In the meantime every open and deregulated economy in the world has watched as prices of its limited and most valuable fixed stock of land and property are inflated by the onslaught of highly mobile global capital flows. Cities such as London, Shanghai, New York, Accra, Nairobi, Lima, Medellín, Frankfurt and Dublin have all attracted global flows of the Casino's capital and watched as local house prices rose inexorably – beyond the reach of millions of their citizens.

The housing market in OECD countries gives the purest expression to Milton Friedman and Anna Schwarz's explanation of the cause of inflation outlined in their *Monetary History of the United States, 1867–1960*. Namely, that inflation is everywhere and always a monetary phenomenon, resulting from and accompanied by a rise in the quantity of money relative to output (*output*, in this case, meaning quantity of property or land).

The global owners of that capital are in a constant search for safe, high-yielding assets (collateral) in which to park their investments, and in ways that will generate (unearned) rent. This search for safe assets has occurred because of a shortage of the very safe public assets – government debt (bonds or gilts) – preferred over property by investors running global asset management funds or insurance companies. As a result, those responsible for investing vast sums of the world's wealth, both individuals and institutions, aim their billions at property markets, which while not as safe as government bond markets are nevertheless considered safer than other assets. Above all, they can be relied upon to generate inflated returns in the form of rent and profits.

Property prices have been blasted into the stratosphere and have been made unaffordable, not because of a shortage of housing supply but by the excess of a potent propellant – finance. And as night follows days, property prices will fall when the propellant is withdrawn and flows of finance decline.

Land: Supply and Demand

Land is treated as if it were a commodity because nothing under capitalism must be allowed to inhibit the formation and operation of markets. Markets must be treated with the respect and awe previously granted by the ancients to mythical gods. Capitalist ideology dictates that markets must be given the awesome power of deciding the value of land as a traded, if fictitious, commodity. Markets, and only markets, must judge who is to be housed and who is to be made homeless. For free market ideologues, there must be no interference; no measure or policy must be countenanced that would influence the brutal decisions of these markets.[17] Neither price, nor supply, nor demand must be fixed or regulated; the only policies and measures in order are those that ensure the market *is the only organising power* in the housing market.

The wider public (those not trained in the current economic ideology) understand full well that their chance of a roof over their heads is not governed by the body created to ensure their security – democratically elected governments – but by something as invisible and capricious as the ancient gods: 'the market'. Many may rightly regard governments and politicians as impotent in the face of market power. That is why, just as in the 1930s, the world's people clamour for protection from the ruthless governance of markets. Their appeals for, among other things, a safe and affordable roof over their heads are frequently dismissed as 'populism'.

In 2024, around 1.6 billion people were estimated to be living without the security of adequate accommodation, a number that could rise to 3 billion by 2040, according to the World Economic Forum.[18] And being unhoused is as much a 'First World' problem as it is a problem for low-income countries. Britain, one of the richest countries in the world, has the highest proportion by far of unhoused people living on the streets and in temporary accommodation.[19] In the 2024 *Annual Homelessness Report*, the US Department of Housing and Urban Development revealed that a total of 771,480 people – or about 23 of every 10,000 people in the United States – experienced homelessness in an emergency shelter, safe haven, transitional housing programme or in unsheltered locations across the country – an historically high number.[20]

In a dataset of fifty-seven countries, 80 per cent have seen increases in housing prices in the last twelve years. Advanced economies, or the most developed countries in the world, have seen the highest increases. But across all measured countries, the real price of housing has increased nearly 30 per cent on average since 2010.[21]

Statistics are rare on how house prices have risen worldwide since the deregulation policies of President Reagan and Prime Minister Thatcher in the 1980s. But one property company has calculated that back in 1980 in England, the average house sold for just £19,273, compared to £239,927 in 2020 – a staggering 1,145 per cent increase.[22]

House prices are now eight times the average annual wage, according to official statistics. The ratio was less than five before 2001.[23] According to the UK's statistics agency, for the poorest households, the average house price in England was 18.2 times above average income in 2022–3, with the affordability threshold being met only by the richest 10 per cent of households, at a ratio of 4.3.[24] Nick Bano explains that in the seventy years between the 1950s and the COVID-19 pandemic, the value of the housing stock in the United Kingdom increased by 500 per cent. In the last of those decades – the ten years between the Global Financial Crisis and the pandemic – the total value rose by £750 million per day.[25]

London was alone among all UK nations and regions in that the average home was defined as unaffordable for all income groups.[26] The cost of the typical property in the capital is equivalent to almost thirty-five years of income for the poorest households and 5.9 times the income of the richest households, above the affordability threshold.[27]

Build More!

Rising prices are blamed on a shortage in the supply of housing. The law of supply and demand, as applied to residential property, requires an expansion in construction to bring prices down.[28] The call goes out from politicians and the media to build more houses, cover the land in ever more concrete, ignore the impact on the environment, channel more taxpayer-funded subsidies and tax breaks to line the capacious pockets of financial institutions and property-owning voters, and protect the interests of political allies in construction and property markets. 'Do everything necessary to increase supply and lower prices' goes the argument made by orthodox economists. Yet despite these heroic efforts by British conservative governments and their allies, increased housebuilding has refused to conform to this law. Even as supply expanded, prices stubbornly continued to rise.

And as Nick Bano argues, it's strange that speculative developers would build homes in order to devalue them, that they would somehow act against their own interests by producing enough surplus housing to bring down the average price.

At risk of making this chapter UK-centric, I would like to introduce readers to the work of Ian Mulheirn currently chief economist at Britain's Department of Transport. Mulheirn has over many years examined data on the British housing stock. He has challenged the commonly held claim that Britain has failed to build enough houses to meet the demand for places to live. On the contrary, he cites official data that show since the 1996 nadir of house prices, the English housing stock has grown by 168,000 units per year on average, while growth in the number of households averaged 147,000 per year.[29] As a result, while there were 660,000 more dwellings than households in England in 1996, this surplus grew to over 1.1 million by 2018. Similar trends were apparent in Scotland and Wales.

This story – based on the official count of dwelling stock and the Labour Force Survey – is also visible in the English Housing Survey and corroborated by alternative measures such as the growth in total residential floor space and bedrooms per head of population. It is just possible that the surplus of housing is in the wrong place or region. But here too, writes Mulheirn, the available data suggest that even in London and the South East the number of houses has grown faster than the household count.[30] This includes the phenomenon of 'second homers' – those able to afford more than one roof over their heads, one of which is invariably empty and unavailable to buyers.

The facts are these: the massive increase in housing costs over the last twenty years has coincided with an expansion in the supply of surplus housing. The increase in the housing stock has had a minimal impact on prices. According to a comprehensive report by Professor Ryan-Collins, estimates of the sensitivity of UK house prices to increases in housing stock consistently show that a '% increase in housing stock delivers only a 1.5–2% reduction in house prices . . . This contrasts with a 306% increase in mean nominal English house prices since January 2000 from £75,219 to £305,370.'[31]

When the fuel of the Global Casino's mobile, private capital is matched by easy if costly mortgage credit and money from both commercial banks and the Bank of Mum and Dad – and in turn supplemented by government subsidies and tax breaks – house prices rise.

The key point is that a financialised housing market tends towards the inefficient use of the housing stock. Households outcompete first-time buyers and others in 'need' of housing and overconsume housing (or under-occupy it) as they purchase it as a financial asset or positional good rather than primarily as a place to live.[32] The result is rising house prices and an increasing surplus of bedrooms and general stock. Liberalised mortgage markets enable this inefficient use of an asset, as existing homeowners can always get bigger mortgages or need smaller deposits.

UK government subsidies to the private rented sector help ratchet up house prices and therefore the value of the housing market as a whole. In Britain it is the law that markets in housing should prevail, and it is the law that puts up rents and ultimately house prices. Nick Bano calls it 'state-backed rent-raising'.[33] Thanks to a Thatcherite law – the 1998 Housing Act – the state's guarantee that landlords can take possession very quickly puts them in an overwhelmingly powerful bargaining position. Under a benefits system first introduced in 1981, the state undertook to pay a portion of the nation's rent. For financially eligible tenants, Housing Benefit paid private landlord rents as they rose. The state guaranteed that a proportion of the working class would always be able to meet those rising costs by underwriting a large part of the national rent bill and providing welfare benefits to match the rising rents.

The main purpose of the Thatcherite recasting of housing rights was to establish the conditions for the creation, and then the constant expansion, of a profitable housing market, writes Bano. The way this was achieved was by regularising the previously unlawful system of cowing tenants into paying more. There was historical precedent for this. Under the Poor Laws, through which local parishes paid the rents of many of the poorest households, a major cause of the massive rent inflation of the early nineteenth century was that 'landlords could be reasonably confident that if they fixed rents too high for the labourer to afford, the parish would indemnify [*sic*]'.[34]

In nineteenth-century writing about housing, rents rise when improvements are made, because those improvements increase the value of the commodity. This still holds true in cities where tenancies are regulated, such as Berlin, Vienna and Copenhagen. But across Britain rents are constantly rising, even as housing conditions are in decline: the government's own figures show that, in 2019, some 13 per cent of privately rented homes (more than half a million) had at least one defect so severe that it posed a serious threat to the tenant's health. Charles Dickens would have found much that is familiar about Britain's modern-day protection of unscrupulous landlords.

The Crisis of Affordability

Counterintuitively for most, building more houses is not the right prescription. The crisis is not one of a housing shortage; it is one of affordability.

There are six keys to making housing more affordable. The first is not to build more market provided housing, but to manage the flow of cash flooding into housing markets. Central banks could deploy macroprudential tools that limit cross-border capital flows and commercial banks could monitor asset prices and introduce policies aimed at restricting certain forms of credit across entire national economies – central banks' so-called macroprudential policies. (Macroprudential approaches are forms of financial regulation whose purpose is to mitigate risk to the financial system as a whole.) The second is for government to impose rent controls on the fictitious market for land, as understood in the broadest sense. The third is for government to build affordable housing that is not subject to market forces. The fourth is to tax property wealth. The fifth is to make it harder or more expensive to buy a second-home or buy-to-let property. The sixth is to allow the mortgages of first-time buyers to be insured or guaranteed by the state, as Ryan-Collins argues.[35]

Maintaining business as usual by building more residential housing without increased regulation, and without providing affordable alternatives to the market, means that prices won't fall: the market will simply absorb more cash. The answer is first to tame and regulate the Global Casino. For it is in this largely unregulated sphere of the global financial system where excessive and inflationary credit creation takes place, credit used to fuel asset prices, including the price of residential housing. However, the globalised system is situated very deliberately beyond the reach of regulatory democracy. Fundamental to its transformation and stabilisation will be the renationalisation of financial systems, with some barriers to the unfettered flow of global capital.

The possibility of such a transformation appears at this time utopian, given the lack of political will and leadership in the top hierarchy of countries, coupled with the extraordinary, if unaccountable power of Wall Street and the shadow banking system. Nevertheless these are issues that must be discussed, because in the event of another global financial crisis, a global war or a catastrophic global climate event, the public will demand answers and a Plan B.

At the national level, governments must use taxation and other policies to *manage* (not control) speculative capital flows. One way of doing this would be for countries to apply a 'Tobin tax' on global financial transactions – a tax of 0.1 per cent levied on every exchange from one currency into another. This small tax casts what Tobin called 'sand in the wheels' of global capital flows and deters short-term currency speculation. Other forms of capital flow management – known as macroprudential policies and instruments – have already been introduced. According to the Bank of England, prudential policies have already been adopted by more than 100 countries.[36] Prudential policies can act both on lenders (banks) in the form of requirements on capital ratios and on borrowers (households) in the form of caps on loan-to-value (LTV) and loan-to-income (LTI) ratios for new mortgages.

The second approach would be to tackle the price inflation in housing markets through the taxation system. First for consideration should be a property speculation tax (PST). This has been applied in Germany, where the tax is levied on the profit resulting from the difference between the purchase price and the sale price of a property, less the costs incurred.[37] This could be used to levy punitive rates on international and homegrown speculators, or those who own second homes and empty properties, encouraging them to invest their cash elsewhere.

Another could be a land value tax (LVT), an annual tax on the incremental increase on the unimproved market value of land that would fall upon the owner of that land.[38] The tax would capture the economic gains deriving from investment by the state or local authorities in, for example, a nearby rail station – gains not due to the landowners' own efforts.

Third, by focusing on national housing markets, we could recognise that not all housing markets are as unbalanced as those of Anglo-American economies. In these markets lending by banks for productive activity is prioritised, as opposed to lending for speculative activity. In other words, domestic banks are incentivised to prioritise lending to businesses over property lending.

A fourth and equally important measure would be to regulate the creation of credit, its allocation and its quantity at domestic level. As Ryan-Collins explains, during their history, almost all central banks have employed forms of formal and informal quantity-based credit regulation under various terms, including 'credit controls', 'credit guidance' or 'moral suasion'.[39] In Japan, Korea and Taiwan, central banks in the decades after the 1940s suppressed the availability of credit for the purchase of land and property, as it was seen to produce excessive asset price inflation.

We know that it is possible to decommodify land. To remove its role as a financial asset and stabilise the housing market worldwide. We know it is possible for the Big State to provide affordable housing to its citizens. All that is needed is wider public understanding of the causes of the global housing crisis, understanding that would hopefully generate the political will for real change to the system of housing – and unhousing – millions of people.

7

Climate and the Casino

Climate breakdown . . . is a giant non-linear outcome generator with wicked convexities. In plain English, there is no mean, there is no average, there is no return to normal. It's one way traffic into the unknown.

Mark Blyth, *Guardian*, 11 August 2021

There is an increasing risk of Planetary Insolvency unless we act decisively. Without immediate policy action to change course, Catastrophic or Extreme impacts are eminently plausible, which could threaten future prosperity.

Institute and Faculty of Actuaries, 16 January 2025

Back in January 2021, Larry Fink, co-founder of the asset management fund BlackRock, told the *Financial Times* that he was sixty-eight years old and had seven grandchildren. 'I want to leave the planet better for them but I am not doing this for environmental reasons – I have a fiduciary responsibility for other people's money and climate change is affecting their investments.'[1]

The Wall Street titan had been horrified to discover that salmon had disappeared from his favourite fishing haunt in Idaho. In 2019, he found that water levels were low in Iliamna Lake in south-west Alaska and that smoke filled the remote landscape. The smoke had obscured the sun, and abnormally high temperatures had sparked wildfires in nearby Siberia. 'The tundra was on fire,' Fink told the *FT*'s Gillian Tett in a video call.[2]

Six years later, on 9 January 2025, Reuters reported that Black-Rock, 'the world's biggest asset manager', would leave the Net Zero Asset Managers Initiative.[3] To be fair, BlackRock had been under attack. In November 2024, the company and rivals were sued by Texas and ten other Republican-led states that claimed Wall Street activism had cut coal production and boosted energy prices. Forced to choose between Texan Republicans and his seven grandchildren, Larry Fink and his company buckled. Yet he, and we, know that climate breakdown poses the gravest threat to the survival of human civilisation and to the stability of what Hamlet called 'this goodly frame, the Earth . . . this brave o'er-hanging firmament' swamped increasingly by a 'foul and pestilent congregation of vapours'.

Today's oligopolistic capitalism is a major cause of the ecological crises we face and why the Global Casino and the ideology that underpins its architecture are unfit to tackle those crises.

Whose Future Is It to Be?

Much of capitalism's preoccupation with the future was theorised by Irving Fisher, a prominent American economist in the early twentieth century. As Liliana Doganova explains, Fisher argued that capitalism has a specific relationship to time.[4] It is resolutely future-orientated, a future in which any entity could engage and hence become capital.

Fisher used the apple tree as an example. The orchard that produces apples (that is, will generate apples in the future) represents capital. But it is the value of the apples, not the tree or the land the orchard rests on, that produces capitalism's real value. As value under capitalism depends only on future capital gains, not present or past gains, the value of the land can be discounted. If apples cannot be profitably sold in the future, then the orchard becomes redundant. Its ancient trees should be ripped up and the land turned over to a 'productive' crop more likely to ensure capital gains in the future.

That formula explains much about capitalism's destruction of nature. Fisher's theory led to a method widely used by firms making investment decisions. The net present value (NPV) of any investment is calculated by projecting the flows of future costs and benefits. However, there is an inherent contradiction in the theory: that flows are then 'discounted' by, for example, a rate of interest, to determine the *present value* of a future sum of money and based on the assumption that a dollar today is worth more than a dollar tomorrow.

While value therefore depends only on the future, at the same time the future is *devalued*. Future time is deemed less worthy than the present *because time has a cost*, according to capitalism. These are just some of the profound contradictions at the heart of capitalism.

Rockhopper, the Adriatic Coast and Discounted Cash Flow Analysis (DCF)

Capitalism's focus on future returns on investment as the only future that matters is well illustrated by the story of oil company Rockhopper Exploration PLC and its failed exploration site at Ombrina Mare near the Adriatic coast of Italy.[5]

The company's drilling project on that stunningly beautiful coast met resistance from the time of its concession in 2008. The concession led to local resistance and massive environmental demonstrations in the Abruzzo region. This was followed by a request for a referendum by ten Italian regions and ultimately by legislative decree that banned near-shore projects like this one.[6] Finally Rockhopper's concession was rejected by the Italian government.

Not that this deterred Rockhopper Exploration, a UK-based company. In 2017, the company launched arbitration proceedings against Italy, demanding compensation for the company's investment in the Ombrina Mare project. The total exploration cost of that investment to Rockhopper and its shareholders was just €2 million. The company had created no infrastructure. There were no oil drilling installations to be dismantled. There were no workers to lay off, no contracts to terminate.

Despite these facts, by using the company's own discounted cash flow (DCF) analysis, the arbitration tribunal awarded Rockhopper €184 million as compensation for the loss of future capital gains, gains that were lost due to popular democratic opposition to oil drilling along the Italian coast.

As Doganova explains, capitalism values the future as relevant temporality for action.[7] In deciding what Rockhopper should be awarded the tribunal looked to the future, not the company's present costs or its past investment. What mattered to the tribunal regarding Ombrina Mare was not what the company invested in its initial exploration, but what capital gains it could have made in the future had that future existed.

To put it bluntly: the tribunal's line of thought was that the future that mattered most was not the real future of the Adriatic coastline or that of its citizens. No, the future that mattered was Rockhopper's imagined future. That is why Rockhopper, the investor whose future imagined profits far outstripped imagined costs (the discounted rate), was awarded €184 million of real money by Italian taxpayers, via their government.

The Rockhopper story illustrates the contradiction at the heart of Fisher's analysis of capitalism's relationship to time. The landmark publication, *The Economics of Climate Change: The Stern Review* helped lay bare that contradiction in 2006.[8] The economist who chaired the review, Nicholas Stern, was alive to the contradiction of using discounting in cost–benefit analysis (CBA) to assess the task of tackling climate and ecological crises. When viewed through capitalism's Fisher lens of discounted cash flow (DCF), ambitious climate policies proved pointless and worthless. The eventual benefits of climate policies were deemed so distant in time they were heavily discounted, and could barely weigh against initial costs, most of which were much more proximate in time.

Stern rejected capitalism's sleight of hand in relation to the future. Instead, the *Stern Review* proposed using discount rates close to zero to make the future count as much as the present, coming to the remarkable conclusion that we must treat the welfare of future generations on a par with our own.

Stern's calculations were attacked by notorious climate denier William Nordhaus, orthodox economist and adviser to the United Nations' Intergovernmental Panel on Climate Change (IPCC).[9] In opposition to Nicholas Stern, Nordhaus argued that 'the discount rate that determines the efficient balance between the cost of emissions reductions today and the benefit of reduced climate damage in the future should be "the return on capital" . . . which measures net yield on investment in capital, education and technology . . . observable in the marketplace . . . and is far higher than the zero-rate applied by Stern.'[10]

Nordhaus is not alone. In 2014, economists advising the UN's IPCC came to the same conclusion:

For most economic sectors, the impact of climate change will be small relative to the impacts of other drivers (*medium evidence, high agreement*).

Changes in population, age, income, technology, relative prices, *lifestyle*, regulation, governance, and many other aspects of socioeconomic development will have an impact on the supply and demand of economic goods and services that is large *relative to the impact of climate change*.[11]

Let me summarise in case the last is not clear: a group of IPCC orthodox economists in a UN report argue that lifestyle impacts on the supply and demand for economic goods would be large compared to the impact of climate breakdown. As another climate economist Professor Steve Keen has explained, forecasts by economists of the economic damage from climate breakdown have been notably sanguine in contrast to the dire warnings by scientists about damage to the biosphere.

Keen explained how economists used three spurious methods to make their own predictions of damages caused by climate change.[12] First, and unbelievably, they assume that about 90 per cent of GDP will be unaffected by climate change, because it happens indoors! In other words, economic activity that takes place inside factories and offices are assumed to be unaffected by floods and other climate shocks. Second, economists use the relationship between temperature and GDP today as a proxy for the impact of global warming over time. Third, they use flawed surveys that diluted extreme warnings from scientists with optimistic expectations from economists.

Keen argues that Nordhaus has misrepresented the scientific literature to justify using a smooth function to describe the damage to GDP from climate change. Correcting for these errors makes it feasible that economic damages from climate change are at least an order of magnitude worse than forecast by economists and may be so great as to threaten the survival of human civilisation.

The Stern report stood apart from the conclusions and economists of the UN's IPCC. Its authors recognised that investment as a cost incurred *now* is vital to avoid and protect against the risks spelled out by scientists of very severe consequences in the future. Today, scientists think we are now well past tipping points, including the burning of the Amazon forest that was once a carbon sink and amid signs we are moving closer to a tipping point for the collapse of the Atlantic Meridional Overturning Circulation (AMOC).[13]

'A lot of discussion is, how should agriculture prepare for this?' scientist René van Westen said. 'But a collapse of the heat-transporting circulation is a going-out-of-business scenario for European agriculture,' he added. 'You cannot adapt to this. There's some studies of what happens to agriculture in Great Britain, and it becomes like trying to grow potatoes in Northern Norway.'[14]

Wall Street Is Gambling with the Future of the Planet

While economists gambled in theoretical terms with our futures, Wall Street gambles in real time. The individuals, financial institutions (like BlackRock, Blackstone, Vanguard) and firms that operate and speculate within the Casino own or manage vast sums of money. These sums have accumulated over time thanks to financial deregulation, pension privatisation, the growth of sovereign wealth funds by oil-exporting countries and the increased prominence of financial speculation within the dynamics of low-taxed and globally mobile capital accumulation.

A fair share of that capital is invested in burning fossil fuels and polluting the planet's atmosphere with toxic emissions.

Urgewald's Global Coal Exit List (GCEL) and Global Oil and Gas Exit List (GOGEL) make up the most comprehensive publicly available database of institutional investments in the oil and gas industry. They show that in May 2024, 5,298 institutional investors (meaning asset management funds, private equity partnership pensions, hedge and insurance funds) were still holding bonds and shares of coal companies that added up to $1.3 trillion.[15] Over 95 per cent of companies on the GCEL list have failed to set a coal exit date and 40 per cent are still planning to develop new coal assets. In addition, 7,291 institutional investors were invested in expanding the oil and gas industry, with a total value of $4.5 trillion. GOGEL shows that 96 per cent of oil and gas producers were still exploring and developing new oil and gas reserves and that the industry had increased its annual capital expenditure on oil and gas exploration by more than 30 per cent since 2021.

The asset management fund Vanguard holds the sad record as the world's biggest fossil fuel investor. The US company holds and manages assets invested in coal, oil and gas companies worth $444 billion. Due to its sheer volume and because it does not have any fossil fuel policy, Vanguard is the number one in fossil fuel investments worldwide. BlackRock, the world's biggest asset management company, is ranked second. Its fossil fuels assets add up to $431 billion, a small proportion of its total financial assets of $11.5 trillion. Saudi Arabia's Public Investment Fund holds fossil fuel assets worth $367 billion and is ranked third by Urgewald, followed by State Street, which holds $184 billion, and Capital Group, which holds $174 billion.

The consequences are well known. According to NASA, 2024 was the hottest year in the recorded history of the planet's temperature.[16] Using World Weather Attribution criteria, a Climate Central 2024 study identified seventy-six extreme heat waves that spanned ninety different countries. Those events put billions of people at risk, including in densely populated areas of South and East Asia, the Sahel, and South America.[17]

These calamities were expected. In 2023, oil and gas production reached a historic high. In the hottest year on record, companies on the Global Oil and Gas Exit List (GOGEL) produced 55.5 billion barrels of oil equivalent (bboe).[18] Global hydrocarbons production surpassed the pre-COVID all-time high.

To address the climate disasters that were a consequence of a heated-up planet, world leaders at the 2023 UN COP conference made total pledges of a pitiful $702 million to the 'Loss and Damage Fund', set aside to support low-income countries in adapting to the climate crisis. Meanwhile the oil and gas industry poured nearly ninety times this amount into searching for new reserves each year. According to GOGEL, upstream companies were spending an average of $61.1 billion on exploration annually.[19]

Shadow Banking and the Global Casino

Because of the wealth they hold and manage, and as explained earlier, individual, corporate and institutional investors cannot deposit their capital in the world's commercial banks. The sums they own or manage far exceed the deposit guarantees of typically $100,000 offered by governments in the event of bank failure. Hence the need to find 'havens' outside the realm of high street banks for investing and protecting the value of vast sums accumulated over time. The 'shadow banking' system is now the gargantuan and dangerously unstable financial behemoth that houses that wealth.

Yet even as they move out of the terrain of commercial main street banking into the financial stratosphere that is shadow banking, institutional investors remain tethered to the real-world banking system. Commercial banks extend loans to hedge funds and other institutional investors in fossil fuels and accept collateral and deposits from those investors. So if there's panic in the shadow banking sector, it quickly infects the world's regulated banks – as governments and central banks witnessed in a series of crises from 2007 onwards. Given their high levels of 'interconnectedness' with the traditional banking system, the shadow banking system and its risky investments pose a systemic risk to real-world financial stability. That is largely because their financing strategies, borrowing (leveraging) and risk-taking are hidden from public scrutiny and regulation.

The 2024 NGO-backed annual report *Banking on Climate Chaos* reviewed only regulated mainstream banks and found that 'the 60 biggest banks globally committed $705 billion to companies conducting business in fossil fuels in 2023'.[20] Five asset managers active in the shadow banking system (what the Financial Stability Board calls the NBFI sector) hold and manage assets in fossil fuel companies worth far more: $1.6 trillion. They also play a critical role in financing fossil industries.

Many of those financial assets include the savings and payments made by millions of workers, entrepreneurs and owners, which are invested in pension and insurance funds. The financial institutions that manage these funds have liabilities, such as future pension payments and insurance policies to pay out, stretching into the future. The race is on therefore to invest savings in assets that will generate sufficient returns ('rent') to meet those liabilities. As things stand, fossil fuels are among the most promising in that regard.

Investment in fossil assets has proved immensely profitable. Whereas renewable projects earn just 5 to 8 per cent on their equity, oil and gas earn more than 15 per cent.[21] Companies active in the shadow banking system and invested in fossil assets include Vanguard, BlackRock, Capital Group and State Street, all of which manage the investments and retirement savings of millions of Americans.

How the State Subsidises and Protects Investment in Fossil Fuels

In addition to these capitalist dynamics we must consider the role of the state in toxic fossil fuel emissions. Governments have deployed fiscal (tax breaks and subsidies) and monetary policies (public credit creation and low, even negative, rates of interest) to support players in the Global Casino, and have used the defence of 'energy security' to do so.

After the Global Financial Crisis, trillions of dollars of low-cost, unconditional credit (debt issuance) was made available by independent central bankers to institutional investors – investment banks, insurance companies, asset management funds, so-called hedge funds, sovereign wealth funds, pension funds and private equity firms – and subsequently used for investment in the fossil fuel sector. As if that 'easy money' were not sufficient, in one year, 2022, public fiscal support for fossil fuels (in the form of subsidies, investments by state-owned enterprises and lending from public financial institutions) exceeded $1.7 trillion globally – a record high.[22]

That helps explain why total financial assets held within the shadow banking system at the end of 2023 rose to an unimaginable $238.8 trillion. Roughly $70 trillion of that total are funds 'authorities have assessed as being involved in credit intermediation activities that may pose bank-like financial stability risks'.[23]

Insurance and Climate Breakdown

At the beginning of 2025, Los Angeles was consumed by wild-fires. California recorded the hottest summer on record in 2024 as climate change dried out the vegetation surrounding Los Angeles. Forests and grasslands were turned into tinder, 'fueling faster, more intense burns', according to Yale Climate Connections.[24] The fires, expected to be among the costliest disasters in US history, deepened a crisis in the state's home insurance market.[25] Due to the rising costs of insurance, thousands in the city had not renewed their household insurance policies, leaving many without adequate fire insurance cover.

'We're marching toward an uninsurable future in this country and across the globe,' wrote Dave Jones in July 2023.[26] Jones served as California's insurance commissioner from 2011 to 2018 and now directs the Climate Risk Initiative at the University of California, Berkeley. It was clear that California's insurance industry was in trouble. The bigger question was this: would that catastrophe increase wider financial stability risks in the Global Casino?

Insurance corporations that manage $40 trillion of the world's insurance premiums – 9 per cent of global financial assets – operate within the non-bank financial intermediary (NBFI) sector.[27] To understand why their activities in the Global Casino pose risks, not just for individuals, households and firms, but also the whole global financial system, let's briefly explore the types of gambling, speculation and leveraging that take place at the heart of the shadow banking system.

In 2023, the IMF investigated potential risks in the NBFI sector. They noted that relatively tight regulations for insurance companies, particularly strict capital requirements, limited the degree to which these companies could invest in riskier assets.

'However,' they explained, 'as insurance companies make extensive use of third-party investment managers, a detailed and timely examination of the actual underlying risk exposures may not always be feasible.'[28] In other words, insurance companies are playing a kind of 'let's hide behind a third party while we play pass the parcel with risky investments.'

Because insurance companies are more fully exposed to climate breakdown than other corporations active in the Global Casino, the following, which may sound a little arcane, is an attempt to explain the tactic used by the sector. The risks that are obscured by insurance companies, according to the IMF, are known as *synthetic leverage*. Investment managers in the insurance sector use these risks to enhance returns.

The European Central Bank explains synthetic leverage as exposure embedded in a third party's derivative contract.[29] Derivatives are complex financial contracts based on the value of an underlying asset, group of assets or a benchmark. Much as the value of an insurance contract depends on the value of an underlying asset, for example, a property in LA's Pacific Palisades. Derivatives managed by others, the IMF argues, could enable an insurance company to take on synthetic (third-party) market exposure (the amount an investor stands to lose should an investment fail), sometimes at little direct cost to the insurance company. This risk allows the company to *amplify gains* if the gamble works, but it may also *magnify losses* if it doesn't.

The IMF cites four case studies of crises where insurance companies were involved that caused 'spillovers' in the broader financial system. First, the UK pension fund and liability-driven investment (the 'Liz Truss mini-budget') episode from 2022 is an example of the interplay of leverage, liquidity mismatches and interconnectedness in the shadow banking sector.

Another example is the financial stress that emerged in Korea's debt markets in October 2022 amid tightening financial conditions and falling property prices. 'The default of a commercial paper issued against real estate project finance loans – a market in which NBFIs such as insurance companies and nonbank credit intermediaries actively participate – set off a broad-based repricing of asset-backed securities, corporate bonds, and short-term notes,' the IMF explains.[30]

The third crisis is the nickel market suspension at the London Metal Exchange in March 2022 caused when commodity-trading firms used commodity-derivative contracts to hedge (speculate) against price declines (of their large inventories). In a volatile market environment, traders can quickly be faced with higher margin requirements when lenders demand the immediate transfer of liquid assets (in particular, cash) as collateral. During the nickel market episode a number of commodity-trading firms cautioned that the liquidity challenges they faced may have threatened their ability to continue supplying commodities to the economy.

The fourth example is the private (unregulated) NBFI credit market, where the IMF reckons rapid growth 'may have increased vulnerabilities in the financial system, with potential systemic implications'. That is because 'lending is largely opaque, driving an accumulation of asset quality performance risks that may be hard for market participants and regulators to discern until it is too late to counteract'. Because of 'the low transparency and limited liquidity in private credit markets', the IMF worries that spillovers to other markets could occur during a stress episode as investors are forced to sell other assets with more timely mark-to-market pricing and more liquid secondary markets in order to access cash.[31]

The Risks of an Uninsurable World

As the Californian wildfires of January 2025 raged, economist Gary Yohe, Huffington Foundation Professor of Economics and Environmental Studies at Wesleyan University, warned that climate change was undermining the insurance systems American homeowners relied on to protect themselves from catastrophes. But, he argued, another threat remained less recognised: the collapse of American insurance systems could pose a threat to the stability of financial markets well beyond the scope of the fires. A dysfunctional property insurance sector could 'create widespread financial instability', he wrote, just as the collapse in the value of opaque bundles of real estate derivatives in 2007–9, which first appeared as 'seemingly localized problems', led to the Global Financial Crisis.[32]

In 2025, the Institute of Actuaries asserted that 'we' must act decisively or else 'catastrophic or extreme impacts are eminently plausible'.[33]

'We' who operate within the boundaries of regulatory democracy are losing that struggle. Instead, a secretive, ruthless billionaire class, operating in the shadows of a globalised financial system and aided by a central bank technocracy, are hurtling us all into a future of catastrophic and extreme impacts. As Professor Trevor Jackson argues, 'we fooled ourselves into thinking that the response to climate change and inequality was in some way going to be a socially egalitarian and democratically decided one, rather than a struggle for control, power and resources.'[34]

If we have been fooled, it is because the billionaire class has conducted their ruthless project of control of the world's power and resources in the shadows, under a system of technocratic, economic impenetrability, and in a language of deliberate unintelligibility. None of the economic balderdash and confused discourse used to conceal the activities of a powerful class amounts to rocket science. In any struggle to save life on earth, we must begin with some understanding of how the powerful have manipulated the great public good that is the world's monetary and financial system – to serve their own selfish, short-sighted and ultimately catastrophic interests.

8

The Need for System Change

The global economic system is out of sync with the biosphere and humanity. It is dangerously over-indebted, has triggered shocking levels of hardship, precarity of existence, inequality of wealth and power relations and is prone to recurring global financial crises, which in turn affect the ecosystem. For humanity and the planet to survive we must radically change the current international financial and economic systems. The world needs system change.

Economic imbalances have had disturbing impacts on the world's political systems, leading to a worldwide wave of nationalism and authoritarianism. The most dangerous effects, however, have been on the planet's ecosystem, on which human survival depends. Capitalism's ruthless and rising levels of extraction and exploitation of the earth's scarce resources have depleted the biosphere and accelerated climate breakdown. It is surely time for economic theory and policy to break out of their narrow confines and their simple, abstract models – blind to the reality of the planet's limits and humanity's condition and devoid of morality, historical context and power relationships. Ricardian economics, popular with economists of both the left and right, cannot address these issues, Nat Dyer explains, as long as the discipline ignores questions of morality, history and power.[1]

In proposing policies for transforming the global economic system we must be clear about goals, strategies and policies. Colin Tudge, a well-known biologist and author of books on evolution, genetics and natural history, including 'enlightened agriculture',[2] suggests we need four tiers to help prepare for a 'twenty-first century renaissance'.

Tier I: Convivial Societies and a Flourishing Biosphere. A key goal for humanity is the creation of 'Convivial Societies – with Personal Fulfilment – and within a Flourishing Biosphere', Tudge writes in *The Great Re-Think*. 'The point is to achieve a balance between society on the one hand, individuals on the other – and the biosphere. Such a goal is far preferable to the policy of limitless "economic growth" . . . The headless chicken pursuit of "economic growth" without moral or ecological guidance, and without a clear and generally acceptable goal in mind, won't do.'[3]

Tier II: Action. Action is everything we as members of society will need to do to transform our world: educating, building, caring, farming, producing, consuming, engineering in all its forms and deploying energy, communications, trade and transport. This book provides only brief signposts for the economic changes needed if the system is to be transformed. Action by readers, citizens and policy-makers will drive change, as they always have done, as distinguished economic historian Barry Eichengreen wrote in the *Financial Times*:

The second Trump administration is a reminder that raw numbers can only take us so far. For as historians will tell you, it is the actions of people, not economies or markets in the abstract, that explain how international currencies rise and fall. It was people who took the crucial steps to build the institutions that made the international dollar. And it is people who will ultimately determine whether these same institutions survive or fail.[4]

Tier III: Infrastructure. The third part of the Great Rethink is the necessity of appropriate infrastructure – provided primarily through governance. For most, this suggests the power of government over economic activity. However, this book shows that governance of both the global and national economies has shifted to private markets in money, land and labour. A restoration of democratic governance can only be achieved via changes to the world's current international infrastructure using economic policy and law to restore democratic oversight and regulation of economies to regions, states and communities. This requires a form of devolution of power, where states are largely self-sufficient but work together with neighbours and allies to achieve international stability.

Changes to national systems require changes to international infrastructure and governance. These in turn require a revival of the spirit of internationalism, as opposed to inward looking, divisive nationalism and autarky (a policy of self-reliance and limited internationalism), with better understanding and communication between nations. People and their nation states will have to learn to agree on common goals and to cooperate in order to devolve power and enact world system change.

Tier IV: Mindset – Towards the Perennial Wisdom. In rethinking the global economic system, Tudge suggests that we need four approaches to shape our world view and arrive at a state he calls 'the perennial wisdom'. These approaches include science, moral philosophy and metaphysics, which asks the 'ultimate questions': what is truth and how do we know what's true, where does 'good' come from, and why are things as they are? Finally, the arts are vital for questioning our assumptions and shaping our attitudes.

A New Mindset: Living Within Our Means

We can also turn to the wisdom of John Maynard Keynes. He held out the promise of a renaissance based on sustainable and self-sufficient economic systems, nested within a framework and spirit of internationalism and the 'oneness of humanity'.[5]

In 1933, the world appeared as grim to Keynes as it appears to us today. Then the international economy had not yet recovered from the Wall Street Crash of 1929 and the Great Depression. Economic policies associated with the gold standard had led to austerity, deflation, unemployment and falling incomes for the world's citizens. Hitler and the Nazi Party were gaining strength in Germany, and war began to seem inevitable.

While the world was less conscious of the threat of climate change, North America was in the middle of an ecological crisis dubbed the Dust Bowl, caused by agricultural erosion of the soils of the Great Plains. It was in this context that Keynes delivered a lecture on national self-sufficiency, by which he meant that societies should learn to live within their means – including their ecosystem means. His insights remain relevant to our predicament today.

Keynes began this lecture with a difficult and humbling confession. He had been wrong about a well-established economic theory, a mistake that he had to acknowledge to free his mind for more radical change. He had been brought up to respect the economic doctrine of free trade, almost as a part of moral law. 'I regarded ordinary departures from it as being at the same time an imbecility and an outrage,' he wrote.[6]

Before Karl Polanyi, Susan Strange or Michael Pettis wrote about the impact of trade wars, Keynes explained in 1933 that it was no longer obvious that countries should dedicate national effort to capturing foreign trade or attracting the finance and power of foreign capitalists. Neither policy offered safeguards and assurances of international peace. In fact, he thought, quite the contrary.

Keynes had read J. A. Hobson's *Imperialism* and so argued against a world economy aimed at the maximum 'cosmopolitanism of capital',[7] regardless of its place of origin. He regarded remoteness between ownership and operation as an evil in the relations between the world's people, an evil more likely to invite political tensions and enmities and undermine the financial calculation behind the scheme. He launched an attack on what we today call 'shareholder capitalism' – the primacy of shareholder interests over all other stakeholders in a company. A form of capitalism that divorced ownership from the real responsibility of management. It made shareholders irresponsible towards what they owned. Worse, it ultimately made managers irresponsible towards shareholders. Thus it was important to domesticate – not globalise – both a nation's economy and responsibility for the economy. The domestication of economic activity led to better outcomes, by focusing on domestic rather than external demand. Living within one's means would be easier when means – like food, housing, health and education – were increased, especially if those means were based on fair distribution and quality rather than quantity. And if all countries were prioritising the domestic economy, international relations would be better balanced too.

In 2025, a Czech billionaire purchased Britain's Royal Mail, first established by King Henry VIII in 1516. This follows foreign ownership of Britain's core infrastructure, including water, sewerage, transport, and energy and fibre networks. Britain's efforts to become self-sufficient in clean energy could be complicated by France's EDF Energy and China's General Nuclear Power Group's ownership of Hinkley nuclear power station, and foreign ownership of Britain's offshore wind capacity. The think tank Common Wealth found that 42.2 per cent of installed capacity from wind farms (both operational and under construction) in the UK is currently owned by foreign public entities such as state-owned enterprises and public pension funds.[8] Danish government entities account for the largest share at 20.4 per cent.

The reason successive British governments have been willing to sell the nation's 'crown jewels' is because Britain, like the United States, has on the one hand a current account deficit, and on the other a capital account surplus, as both countries are magnets for global finance. The inflow of capital from billionaires like Daniel Křetínský (EP Group) helps the UK government settle the 'balance of payments' and enables Britons to maintain their present standard of living. However, such exposure to foreign ownership makes Britain vulnerable to pressure by foreign, possibly hostile, governments. That is why Keynes considered 'remoteness between ownership and operation as an evil' in the relations between the world's people.

The Rate of Interest – and Why It Matters to the Domestication of the Economy

The ability to manage and lower interest rates to support domestic enterprise and industry, as well as to regulate credit creation and prevent the rise of unpayable debts, depends on *(a)* finance being primarily national and *(b)* the reorientation of central bank policy towards the interests of the domestic economy. At present central bankers set policy to defend the value of the currency from globally mobile speculators. These efforts mean that central bankers bow to the interests of investors and speculators in private, global capital markets rather than to domestic interests. That must change.

Higher rates of interest suit bankers and creditors very well. It is how they make money, effortlessly. But high rates of interest, long considered as usurious by all the major faiths, damage the ability of governments, domestic firms and households to borrow to supplement their incomes and invest in sound economic activity.

After the crisis of the global COVID-19 pandemic, central banks raised interest rates. The assumption was that this was done as a way of taming global inflation driven by the 'remoteness between ownership and operation' of the world's overly long supply chains. However, in the case of Britain, the Bank of England did so in order to dampen wage demands. Yet lower wages could not fix interruptions in long supply chains. The effect of the higher rates was to worsen economic activity that was already slowing and to cause a crisis in Britain's shadow banking system and therefore the global financial system.[9]

The first to fall was the UK's gilt market in the Liz Truss turmoil of September 2022, but much worse was to come for the conventional banking sector. In 2023, high rates killed off a range of US banks, including Silvergate Bank, Silicon Valley Bank and Signature Bank, followed by the implosion of First Republic Bank, taken over by JPMorgan Chase. In Europe, the huge and long-standing Credit Suisse bank collapsed.[10] 'A great institution with a history stretching back to 1856 imploded in public view', wrote the *Financial Times*. 'As a Swiss bank, it was meant to be a paragon of safety and secrecy.'[11]

The outburst of global inflation showed up the impotence of both central bankers and politicians in the face of damaging rates of inflation. There can be little doubt that high inflation helped spread disillusionment with the Democratic Party in the months before the election of Donald Trump in 2024.

The fact is that power over key levers in the economy – the exchange rate, the interest rate, levels of investment – had long been transferred away from democratic states and economies and granted to unaccountable global markets in money. No wonder politicians are impotent; no wonder citizens are disillusioned with politics.

High, Real Rates of Interest and the Earth's Finite Resources

Throughout his academic career, Keynes was convinced of the importance of the rate of interest to the management, or mismanagement, of economies. Today, we know that interest when compounded not only has a usurious impact on society, it depletes the earth's finite resources. To repay the compounding cost of interest on any investment requires governments, firms and individuals to accelerate the exploitation and extraction of the land – in the broadest sense of the term – but also labour. For countries to repay foreign debts, forests are stripped, seas are fished and land degraded.

Interest is the 'price' paid on the effortless creation of credit by those who have the power to create credit. Because the creation of credit is effortless, the rate of interest ought to remain low. If the price of socially constructed credit is left to the market, it will be raised to levels that will soon become unbearable for debtors (who lack economic power) and destructive of nature's finite resources.

Geoff Tily is an economist preoccupied with the distortion of Keynes's economic theory by mainstream economists. He insists that Keynes's overwhelming priorities were domestic monetary (not fiscal) policies (and interest rates above all); and second, the architecture of the international monetary system, to make it possible for governments to prioritise domestic monetary policy.

For Keynes, as Tily explains, 'the solution to the class struggle was not the abolition of the market system or private property in Communist Revolution, but . . . the abolition – with a choice only over the pace – of usury within the market system'.[12]

In the closing chapter of *The General Theory of Employment, Interest and Money*, Keynes discussed how his theory would lead to '*the euthanasia of the rentier*, and consequently, the euthanasia of the cumulative oppressive power of the capitalist to exploit the scarcity-value of capital'.[13]

Keynes, unlike so many contemporary economists, understood money not as a commodity, or like a commodity, but as credit – dispensed, at a price, by creditors.

> *Interest today rewards no genuine sacrifice, any more than does the rent of land*. The owner of capital can obtain interest because capital is scarce, just as the owner of land can obtain rent because land is scarce. *But whilst there may be intrinsic reasons for the scarcity of land, there are no intrinsic reasons for the scarcity of capital.*[14]

Keynes realised that countries at different levels of economic development needed different interest rates – but this was not possible under a system of economic imperialism and the geographical diffusion of capital 'embracing the free movement of capital and of loanable funds as well as of traded goods'.[15] Today, President Erdoğan of Turkey, who has relentlessly interfered in the decisions of the Turkish central bank in desperate efforts to keep interest rates low, would do well to learn that lesson. Low rates appropriate to the domestic economy are not possible in a financially globalised world. Globally mobile speculators can use a country's competitive struggle for capital to gang up on, for example, the Turkish lira and force up rates as the price of the currency's stability. Under today's 'dollar standard' there are few means for governments to mitigate economic distress at home, except through what Keynes called 'the competitive struggle for markets . . .'[16] Only if 'nations can learn to provide themselves with full employment by their domestic policy there need be no important economic forces calculated to set the interest of one country against that of its neighbours.'[17]

Austerity as the Wrong Answer to Correcting Imbalances

Austerity was as fashionable among orthodox economists in the nineteenth century as it is in the twenty-first century. Keynes complained that instead of using society's vastly increased material and technical resources to build a 'wonder-city', politicians preferred to build slums, because slums 'paid' whereas the wonder-city would, they thought, have 'mortgaged the future'.

> The same rule of self-destructive financial calculation governs every walk of life. We destroy the beauty of the countryside because the unappropriated splendours of nature have no economic value. *We are capable of shutting off the sun and the stars because they do not pay a dividend.* London is one of the richest cities in the history of civilisation, but it cannot 'afford' the highest standards of achievement of which its own living citizens are capable, because they do not 'pay'.[18]

And as if addressing Colin Tudge, agroecologist and founder of the Real Farming movement in Britain, Keynes argued in 1933 that 'we have until recently conceived it a moral duty *to ruin the tillers of the soil and destroy the age-long human traditions attendant on husbandry, if we could get a loaf of bread thereby a tenth of a penny cheaper'.*[19]

Keynes was advocating national self-sufficiency but warned that some countries might not be a 'large enough unit geographically, with sufficiently diversified natural resources, for more than a very modest measure of national self-sufficiency to be feasible'. In that case, the way should be prepared for regional agreements between countries to serve as an appropriate vehicle for policies of self-sufficiency.

But the core of his case was that he sympathised with those who would minimise rather than maximise economic entanglement between nations: 'Ideas, knowledge, science, hospitality, travel – these are the things which should of their nature be international. But let goods be homespun whenever it is reasonably and conveniently possible, and, above all, let finance be primarily national.'[20]

What Economic Policies Could Help Build 'a Convivial Society Within a Flourishing Biosphere'?

The following areas of major economic policy-making will be necessary if states are to begin anew the construction of a new international financial system, arrived at through international agreement, cooperation and coordination, to meet the goal of 'convivial societies within a flourishing biosphere'.

The domestication of finance. 'Above all, let finance be primarily national.' In other words, the redesign and development of the international economic system to enable states to achieve a degree of self-sufficiency in the production, pricing and distribution of money.

Mobile capital flows are a function of the globalisation of finance. They are designed to be beyond the reach of governments, especially democratic governments. That much Friedrich Hayek made clear in his famous text *Denationalisation of Money*.[21] But global mobile money flows, like global inflation, can destabilise not just national economic systems, but also the global geopolitical system if elected politicians are stripped of power to manage cross-border capital flows. In 2025, we witnessed just such a global movement towards nationalism and protectionism – a reaction to waves of global mobility, financial instability and inflation.

Constraints on capital mobility. To achieve self-sufficiency and autonomy in policy-making and to end speculation and currency volatility, there must be limitations on global capital mobility. Taxes designed to throw 'sand in the wheels' of footloose capital can restore monetary and exchange rate stability to states.

In his book *Moneyland: Why Thieves and Crooks Now Rule the World and How to Take It Back*, Oliver Bullough shared an illuminating analogy of the way in which unregulated capital flows lead to global systemic financial crises. His analogy begins with the international financial system that prevailed during the crises of the 1930s.

To understand how the system worked, imagine an oil tanker, a ship full of oil.

If a tanker has just one huge tank, then the oil that fills it can slosh backwards and forwards in ever greater waves, until it destabilises the vessel, which overturns and sinks. That was the system after the First World War, when the waves of speculative money capsized democracy.

At Bretton Woods the delegates designed a new kind of ship, where the oil was divided up between many smaller tanks, one for each country. The ship held the same volume of oil, but in a different way. The liquid could slosh back and forth within its little compartments but would not be able to achieve enough momentum to damage the integrity of the entire vessel.

And if one compartment sprang a leak, then it wouldn't threaten the whole cargo. It was possible to move oil from one compartment to another but (at the risk of pushing this metaphor to the point of absurdity) you needed permission from the captain, and the money had to go through the ship's official plumbing.[22]

Note how Bullough makes the immediate connection between 'waves of speculative money' and 'capsized democracy'. Before and after both the Global Financial Crisis of 2007–9 and the COVID-19 crisis, waves of speculative money gradually capsized Western democracy.

The key point of Bullough's story is that for the global financial and monetary system to be stable, all the sailors, or states, on board the proverbial tanker must participate in the system – cooperating to manage the smaller compartments and keep the whole tanker stable. That explains why the only way to tame the power of the Global Casino is to contain flows of capital between compartments, or states.

The Trump 2025 economic plan and a market access charge. As I write this book, the possibility of international cooperation and coordination is a pipe dream. It was torpedoed by the President of the United States, Donald Trump, who was determined to make enemies of as many foreign states as possible. The principle of international cooperation and coordination to serve the interests of the American public appears alien to him and to most of the autocratic, nationalist and even fascist leaders now at the helm of the economies of their countries.

However the possibility of 'containing' capital entering the United States has become very real under Trump's leadership. In

November 2024, the man who was to become Trump's chief economic adviser, Stephen Miran, published an article suggesting that just as President Trump proposed to introduce tariffs on goods entering the United States, so he may soon impose tariffs on capital flowing into the country. [23]

In 2019, US Democrat Senator Tammy Baldwin and Republican Senator Josh Hawley published a bill that called for taxes on capital inflows and for a weak dollar policy. Then in 2025, conservative think tank Compass (US) published a report: *Implement a Market Access Charge (MAC)*. The think tank claims to be 'developing a conservative economic agenda to supplant blind faith in free markets with a focus on workers, their families and communities, and the national interest'.[24]

Compass argued that foreigners were not trading their goods for US goods and products. Instead they were trading products for US financial assets, including corporate equity, real estate and Treasury debt. The think tank proposed a charge (tax) on 'foreign purchases of dollar-denominated American financial assets, starting at a rate of 50 basis points, [which] would increase by 50 basis points every year (or six months) until a trade balance or surplus is achieved'.[25] The charge would then decrease the year after a surplus is achieved. The MAC would be collected automatically and electronically on all foreign capital inflows by the computer systems already present in the US banks that handle most of America's cross-border financial transactions. Compass proposed that rather than succumbing to a 'blind faith in free markets', the American state should manage cross-border capital flows.

Trade wars are often depicted as a conflict between countries. But as Klein and Pettis argue in their acute analysis of the global economy, *Trade Wars Are Class Wars*, a conflict *within* a country is often transposed wrongly (and often deliberately) as a conflict *between* countries.[26]

The assumption that America's declining economic power was down to the wicked trading strategies of foreigners led millions of Americans to vote for Trump, the candidate promising to impose tariffs that would 'make America great again'. Many voted in the hope his administration would improve living standards, tame ill-defined 'elites' and end policies for equality and diversity that, it was argued, deprived everyday Americans of decent incomes and job security.

Few understood that it was the nature of the deregulated international financial and trading system that had led to job and income losses in the United States. They were not alone. That misunderstanding was shared by most mainstream economists and politicians. As Trump's economic adviser notes, voters were ahead of the game. Among voters, if not among economists, he explained, the consensus underpinning globalisation has frayed, and both major parties have taken on policies that aim at boosting America's position within it.[27]

America's trade war is a conflict between an alliance of rich exporters, wealthy Wall Street individuals and firms on one side and, on the other, the nearly 9 million Americans who maintain their livelihoods by holding multiple jobs and the 80 per cent of Americans who live from one pay cheque to another.[28] Those inequalities have long fuelled political tensions and led to the growth of populist political parties.

The tragedy is that the president, while supposedly conducting a trade war to protect the interests of Americans, was in fact running a business – the Trump Media & Technology Group – and using the prestige and power of the White House to enrich himself and his family.

Could the US lead a transformation of the global economy?

It is difficult to predict the outcome of Trump's chaotic trade and economic policies, but I have long believed the United States would, in the event of a threat to its economy, be the first to introduce controls over mobile speculative capital, and thereby lead the transformation of the international financial system away from its current state of disorder. However, Trump's criminality and the profound contradictions in his administration's approach to global trade arrangements, coupled with his determination to make as many enemies as possible, means the time for transformation has not yet arrived.

As Klein and Pettis argue, the United States will lose the wider trade war if its politicians fail to understand (or choose not to understand) the role of Wall Street in fuelling trade wars and to take action to curtail Wall Street's power. Current account (trade) imbalances can only be stabilised by addressing the issue of the country's open capital account and the strong US dollar. The reasoning is as follows: As long as trade surplus countries (like China and European countries), the world's central banks, and corporate and individual investors and speculators are all free to re-invest their earnings (savings) by buying intangible American financial assets (for example, US Treasury bonds, stocks and shares, derivatives), the US dollar will remain strong and the US current account unbalanced. Inflows of capital into US financial markets strengthen the US dollar. A strong dollar makes US exports more expensive and imports cheaper. That in turn explains America's (and other) unsustainable trade deficits.

Why do foreign governments and firms buy US financial assets that have earned dollars by selling goods into the US market? The answer is that under the current international system, central banks have no choice: they are expected to hold US Treasury bills (debt) as reserves, just as they once held gold as an indication of their wealth and credibility. In addition, for most countries, only US dollars can be used for the purchase of oil, gas and pharmaceuticals. For other investors, the US has deep capital markets with many advantages: their investments are secure, contracts are upheld by a transparent and (so far) sound legal system and investment in US financial assets is hugely profitable.

That helps explain why the US trade imbalance is so lucrative for Wall Street. Any foreign institution, firm or individual wanting to use their earnings from trade to buy an American financial asset does so via Wall Street. If the foreign institution needs to borrow to buy an American asset, Wall Street has a loan to sell them. If they need US dollars to finance the purchase of US stocks and shares, Wall Street can arrange the currency exchange. If they need to buy US Treasury bills (debt securities), Wall Street has a brokerage that can help.

Wall Street has a very big stake in the business of selling American financial assets to foreign institutions and will be resistant to changes that undermine that profitability, even if those changes are good for the jobs and incomes of Americans – and result in an end to trade wars.

Are these plans realistic for the world's hyperglobalised economies tackling 'polycrises'?
Far from being radical, decisions by nation states to manage their economies, to exercise national sovereignty in monetary matters and over their capital and current accounts are both democratic and, in economic terms, entirely reasonable. But are they realistic in this digital age of hyperglobalisation and polycrises? There will be ferocious resistance in the United States to the effective taxation of capital inflows by Wall Street and by foreign financial centres like the City of London, Frankfurt and Hong Kong.

There will be even greater resistance if the tax on inflows is coupled with a tax on outflows by citizens and foreigners. Until, that is, the globalised system implodes again, causing catastrophic economic failure, high levels of unemployment and bankruptcies and political unrest. Even worse, current global political and economic tensions could easily collapse into global warfare.

If the global economy were to collapse again, then Wall Street and other owners of footloose capital would, we confidently predict, plead with governments and taxpayers for bailouts, protection and guarantees against losses.

There have been at least two such economic catastrophes in the brief quarter century before 2025: once after the Global Financial Crisis of 2007–9 and again during the COVID-19 crisis. After the COVID-19 crisis, governments failed to work together to alleviate the economic and social repercussions of the crisis. Above all, central banks bailed out Wall Street and the City of London almost unconditionally. Far from curtailing their speculative activities, the bailouts consolidated the power of these financial centres and led most players in the crisis to believe they were too big to fail and too big to jail.

Taxation and Wealth

Restraints on capital movements must be used by states to tax all citizens fairly. Such management of mobile capital flows will enable states to tax *all* mobile multinational financial corporations and wealthy individuals on the same terms as firms and individuals tied to the domestic economy.

Above all, taxation must be applied to the super-rich, who have always found ways to avoid paying taxes. Capital mobility allows the wealthy to transfer their capital gains to tax havens, away from where the gains are earned. As Rogé Karma explains, the super-rich do not earn wages or salaries.[29] Comparisons of incomes do not show up the disparities in wealth. Instead wealth is derived from the ownership of assets that tend to appreciate (or not) over time. They include stocks and shares, property, works of art, financial assets, yachts and private jets. Karma writes:

> Elon Musk hasn't taken a traditional salary as CEO of Tesla since 2019; Warren Buffett, the chair of Berkshire Hathaway, has famously kept his salary at $100,000 for more than 40 years. Their wealth consists almost entirely of stock in the companies they've built or invested in. The tax-law scholars Edward Fox and Zachary Liscow found that even when you exclude the 400 wealthiest individuals in America, the remaining members of the top 1 per cent hold $23 trillion in assets.[30]

Unlike wages, which are taxed when they are earned, assets are only taxed when they are sold, or 'realised'. The authorities justify this on the grounds that the assets only exist on paper – and cannot be taxed until they are sold for cash. The rich, therefore, do not sell their assets. Instead, they use assets as collateral for additional leverage or borrowing. The loans are not considered income, because at some point they must be repaid – *so they too are not taxed*.

A Forbes analysis found that, as of April 2022, Musk had pledged Tesla shares worth more than $94 billion, which 'serve as an evergreen credit facility, giving Musk access to cash when he needs it'. The benefits of assets as leverage for raising additional finance are huge.

It gets worse. According to Karma, a provision of United States tax code known as 'stepped-up basis' – or, more evocatively, the 'angel of death' loophole – means that when an individual dies, the value of assets gained during their lifetime becomes immune to taxation. Those assets can then be sold by the billionaire's heirs to pay off any outstanding loans without having to worry about taxes.

A 2021 ProPublica investigation of the private tax records of America's twenty-five richest individuals found that they collectively paid an effective tax rate of just 3.4 per cent on their total wealth gain from 2014 to 2018. Elon Musk paid 3.3 per cent, Jeff Bezos 1 per cent, and Warren Buffett – who has famously argued for imposing higher income tax rates on the super-rich – just 0.1 per cent.

The failure to tax wealth is at the heart of today's global inequality and of many political insurrections. For the sake of social and political justice, that must change.

Taxation and the Carbon and Finance Sectors

Capital mobility allows big 'natural resource' and financial corporations and wealthy individuals to evade taxation – a major loss of revenue for governments. This loss undermines the power of the state to manage public finances and fund investment in the economy. Management of cross-border capital flows will make it harder for gamblers to sweep their profits and capital gains out of country A, where profits are taxed, into country B, which operates as a tax haven.

In 2021, an ambitious international tax reform of corporations was agreed to by the G20 group of countries – expanded with time to include 138 jurisdictions. According to the OECD, the agreement on 'domestic tax base erosion and profit shifting (BEPS)' equips governments with rules and instruments to address tax avoidance by big corporations, ensuring profits are taxed where economic activities generating them take place, and where value is created. This was an encouraging development, especially as it required and enabled international coordination and cooperation.

However, and according to the IMF, the agreement covers just over 100 very large multinational corporations with turnover of at least €20 billion – and excludes the natural resource and financial sectors. In a globalised economy weighed down by more than $450 trillion in financial assets, a €20 billion gain for 138 countries is tiny.[31]

As the IMF explains, global corporate income tax revenue is estimated to rise by about 6 per cent (0.15 per cent of GDP) at the cost of some investment decline. This revenue effect could be larger in the long run as pressures from tax competition and profit shifting abate. Country-specific effects are hard to gauge, but will likely be negative in some investment hubs. Developing countries will likely gain, but effects are modest in relation to their large revenue needs for development. Only constraints and conditionality attached to capital mobility will require those in the big oil and gas ('natural resource') and financial sectors to honour obligations to pay taxes in the domains in which they make capital gains and profits.

Are Central Bankers Really Independent?

While private financial institutions were protected and bailed out after both crises, there were few conditions attached to the bailouts. The events were not used as opportunities to hold financiers and global corporations (like that run by Masayoshi Son) accountable for dangerous speculation and high levels of leverage (debt) and to impose conditions and regulation that would prevent future gambling on borrowed money and its consequence: financial crisis. Instead, the two financial crises simply consolidated the power of Wall Street and other finance centres and concentrated economic power in central bank technocrats.

After the crises, public civil servants – the staff of central banks – were forced to adopt unconventional and previously unthinkable policies in their attempts to stabilise private global capital markets. As Joscha Wullweber explains in *Central Bank Capitalism: Monetary Policy in Times of Crisis*, central bankers became unelected governors of the globalised financial system.[32] Their efforts failed. Instead of stabilising the deregulated international system, the reverse occurred. Central bank policies and actions after the COVID-19 crisis made the system more unstable. Central bankers strengthened, rather than tamed, the prime source of instability: the shadow banking system of excessive credit and debt creation.

Yet the actions and decisions of central bankers were not and are not subject to parliamentary debate or voting procedures, despite the far-reaching implications of their decisions. Instead, central bankers are treated as if they're maestros of finance, the term associated with one of history's most unsuccessful central bankers – Alan Greenspan, chair of the Federal Reserve (1987–2006). In the run-up to the Global Financial Crisis, Greenspan and his board failed to understand, foresee and forestall what was to be a catastrophic economic crisis for the people of the United States and the world. A crisis that I believe sowed the seeds of the authoritarian regimes in place today. Central bankers are not apolitical, technocratic and neutral in their decision-making. To expect them to be so is to disregard human frailty.

However, central bankers today face a dilemma. Should they use all their resources to maintain the financial stability of the Global Casino? Or should they instead focus on expanding sustainable investment, employment and prosperity at home, in the domestic economy? They cannot do both, although the Federal

Reserve of the United States is mandated to try. Most central bankers tend towards serving the interests of global capital markets until financial crises force them to respond to the needs of the real economy.

To avert further financial crises, governments must mandate central banks to use both their immense power and the unlimited financial resources at their disposal to manage, stabilise and discipline the international monetary and financial system. In other words, to tame and regulate capital mobility. These actions are necessary if central bankers are to both prevent and manage global crises – including ecological crises. Above all, those powers must be used in service of the domestic economy, not the private globalised economy.

An Alternative to the Hegemonic US Dollar as the World's Reserve Currency

To replace the imbalances caused by international dependence on a single hegemonic currency, a new international 'clearing union' for settling trade payments between states is proposed. A multilateral clearing union could be designed to *(a)* replace the concept of a single currency as the basis for all international trade payments and *(b)* to encourage sustainable and balanced levels of trade between all countries, not just those with access to hard currency. The economists Massimo Amato and Lucio Gobbi argue that despite appearances, the hegemony of the US dollar has already begun to weaken.[33] The fading of the dollar's star brings to mind, they suggest, a comment in Thomas Mann's novel *Buddenbrooks*:

> The outward signs, the visible, tangible ones, of fortune and ascent only manifest themselves when the downward parabola

has actually begun. Those outward signs need time to come to us, like the light of one of the stars up there, of which we do not know whether it is about to go out or whether it is already extinguished when it shines at its brightest.[34]

There was a time when the global monetary system based on the US dollar seemed eternal and unchanging. And sure enough, despite recurring crises, the dollar system, like a bright shining star, still illuminates global financial markets. But we must not allow ourselves to be blinded by a light that may be dimming and that no longer corresponds to the harmony of the world.

The adoption of the US dollar as the world's reserve currency at the 1944 Bretton Woods conference was on the insistence of a British economist, Dennis Robertson, with the backing of American delegates.[35] Robertson was hostile to Keynes's theories and his plans for post-war economic stabilisation. At the Bretton Woods conference, he, not the Americans, happened to be responsible for an amendment to the Final Act of the Bretton Woods Articles of Agreement that ensured the 'criteria of payment of official gold subscription (to the System) should be expressed as official holdings of gold and United States dollars'.[36] As Ed Conway notes, what had sparked Robertson's intervention remains something of a mystery – though he appears to have done it off his own back, and against Keynes's advice:[37]

> The problem was that by equating the dollar with gold, the agreement set in place a kind of mini-gold standard for one currency. The dollar was formally enshrined as being directly convertible into gold, which contributed both to its dominance over other currencies and to the ultimate collapse of the Bretton Woods system in the 1970s.[38]

Keynes had as early as 1943 developed a far more sustainable plan, one that would have prevented the dominance of any single currency over international trading relationships. As he explained to members of Britain's House of Lords, the main object of his plan for an International Clearing Union (ICU) was this: 'to provide that money earned by selling goods to one country, can be spent on purchasing the products of another country. In jargon, a system of multilateral clearing. In English, a universal currency valid for trade transactions in all the world.'[39]

Keynes's plan – which is still the best alternative to the dominance of the US dollar or any other hegemonic currency – was modelled on the relationship between commercial banks and the central bank, a system that operates in all countries with developed banking systems. Under this plan, each participating country would have an account with the clearing union, much as a commercial bank has an account with a central bank. Central banks provide commercial banks with a daily overdraft of central bank reserves to help balance the millions of transactions that take place each day when customers remove money (for example, a mortgage) from Bank A into Banks B or C. The central bank's reserves act as a temporary balancing item while transactions are settled between banks, and their books balanced. But reserves can only be used within the central bank system – they cannot be used outside in the real economy.

In just the same way, a new international clearing union would create a 'money' – Keynes called it 'Bancor' – that could only be used within the International Clearing Union and that would act as an overdraft to help balance the books of Country A earning money by selling goods to Country B and then using that money to buy commodities from Country C. Countries would be granted overdrafts proportional to the scale of their international trade, but 'every country in the world would stand possessed of a reasonable share of that currency proportional to its needs'.[40]

Countries would be disciplined (with higher interest rates charged on their overdrafts) if they built up a trade deficit and would be punished just as severely if they built up a trade surplus. The system would encourage countries to find outlets for their surplus production and to import the surplus of neighbouring or allied countries. They would manage and expand their trading arrangements to maintain a balanced system.

Keynes's proposal for international cooperation and coordination in constructing an ICU was, according to his own judgement at the time, an 'ideal scheme . . . complicated and novel and perhaps Utopian'.[41] Given the crisis we face today, precipitated by the strong US dollar and the associated trade imbalances, the plan no longer seems utopian. Many have proposed the use of alternative currencies to the US dollar – such as the Chinese yuan. That would simply transfer power over the world's trading arrangements to another hegemonic state.

Keynes's plan is in fact the answer to the dystopian age we are currently living through. An International Clearing Union would be a far more sustainable system for managing trade transactions between nations. Such a clearing union could perhaps take place first at a regional level. Africa is a prime candidate for such a clearing union.[42]

Africa, the US dollar and the vast financing challenge of decarbonisation

Africa suffers unnecessarily from the actions of the world's issuer of the global reserve currency. Its net commodity exporters lost substantial value in 2022 mainly due to monetary policy tightening by the United States' Federal Reserve. Once again, the continent is facing a range of sovereign debt crises – debt denominated in US dollars – that are set to become solvency, not liquidity, crises in the near future.

By providing the framework of a multinational structure for clearing payments, an African Payments Union (APU) would enable and require African countries to make cross-border payments in their own currencies. The clearing process would change the ownership of reserves and permit exchange rates to increase or decrease within a given range and a set period, in response to changes in reserve levels, explains Jane D'Arista in *All Fall Down*.[44] When approved by a supermajority of its members, the APU could act as an international lender of last resort by creating credit as central banks do – a role the IMF cannot play given its dependence on taxpayer contributions.

Keynes did not believe that humanity had the capacity to overcome differences and unite behind a proposal for trade stability, harmony and peace. But in 1944 there was little awareness that the world could collapse into a 'climate abyss' that threatens the very survival of human civilisation. Today, we cannot say we did not know. Furthermore, as the BRICS debate on de-dollarisation has shown, geopolitical tectonic plates are shifting, and the dollar's star is dimming.

The proposal is that African leaders unite behind a harmonious, continent-wide trading and payments system that will help countries share investment, projects and innovation for tackling the climate crisis. This plan would unite the continent while respecting the political and economic autonomy of Africa's fifty-five states and would help build social, political and ecological resilience for future generations.

This may sound a radical proposition given the political, economic and cultural differences of the great continent that is Africa. However, Professor Massimo Amato of Bocconi University and

Lucio Gobbi of Trento University argue this (in an unpublished paper shared with the author):

> The good news is that such a collaborative alternative is already in the process of construction at a regional level and is both technically and politically feasible . . . One such arrangement is M-Bridge, a payments infrastructure using blockchain technology and sponsored by the Bank for International Settlements (BIS).

In addition, an African cross-border payments system already exists – the Pan-African Payment and Settlement System (PAPSS) – intended to support the African Continental Free Trade Area (AfCFTA). The explicit goal of PAPSS is to enhance commercial integration between African states along the lines of the African Continental Free Trade Agreement.

Compared to inter-European trade, inter-African trade is currently well below its economic potential and the politically desirable level. PAPSS could help ensure that inter-African trade becomes the trigger for a shift from low-value-added sectors towards a manufacture-based economy – just as happened in Europe under the European Payments Union, when the continent recovered from the devastation of the Second World War.[44]

These systems achieve three important goals. First, they are payment platforms. Second, they are liquidity-saving mechanisms (in the sense that they reduce dependency on US dollars and euros). Third, they are financing tools for regional traders, individuals, firms, banks and states.

The continent has another great advantage. The African Union, with headquarters based in Ethiopia, speaks with one voice at big international meetings such as those of the G20 (where it is a permanent member), the European Union and the

World Health Organization. Latin America, in stark contrast, is divided. It is not represented as a bloc in these international forums. In addition, Africa already has multiple regional trade blocs, including the Community of Sahel–Saharan States (CENSAD), the Common Market for Eastern and Southern Africa (Comesa), the East African Community (EAC) and the Economic Community of West African States (ECOWAS).

A Progressive Way Forward for Democratic Nations?

As I have tried to show, the global economy is complex and ungovernable as a single entity. Managing the 'tanker' of global capital requires decentralisation into 'compartments' – that is, states – exercising power over markets in money, goods and services. It would lead to the shortening instead of lengthening of all supply chains, and many other changes besides.

Decentralisation of economic power and a return to the philosophy of 'living within our means' are fundamental to the functioning of democratic governments, but also to the stability of the climate and the restoration of the biosphere. But decentralisation is also sound for the functioning of an international system of fair trade and finance. In *Taking Back Control?* Wolfgang Streeck reminds readers of the work of the political scientist, economist and system theorist Herbert Simon. Simon explained that complex systems can be made governable by division into subsystems, with each absorbing a part of the overall complexity and handling it internally.[45]

Decentralisation is vital for building the resilience of societies and economies faced with climate breakdown and ecosystem collapse. As Phila Back argues, all life is a unity – a fundamental concept of ecology. Fungi, part of the 'wood-wide web', 'are entirely decentralized and essentially unbounded branching threads that intertwine and bond with other organisms to exchange and transmit substances as well as information across extensive underground networks.' Furthermore, as Back explains, 'fungi hold promise for resolving some of our most pressing environmental problems, as they can detoxify contamination, accelerate regeneration of devastated landscapes and sequester atmospheric carbon on a potentially very large scale'.[46] The economics profession has a lot to learn from fungi.

Acknowledgements

Sincere gratitude is difficult to convey, but I owe an immense debt to the friends and colleagues who advised and commented on this book. I have for many years benefited from the sage counsel and guidance of the monetary theorist and macroeconomist Geoff Tily, author of *Keynes Betrayed*. While any errors in the book are entirely mine, the following provided comments, corrections and amendments that helped me avoid some, if not all, pitfalls: Richard Kozul-Wright, Josh Ryan-Collins, Myriam Vander Stichele and Maz Kessler. My greatest debts are to economists no longer with us, including J. M. Keynes and Victoria Chick, and to the political economists Karl Polanyi and Susan Strange. The book draws on the work of many brilliant economists, including Michael Pettis, Jane D'Arista, Daniela Gabor, Kari Polanyi Levitt and Geoffrey Ingham.

I would also like to thank my publisher at Verso, Leo Hollis, for his unwavering belief in my work, and for the patient diligence of my editors, Mark Martin and Joy Hoppenot.

Finally, my partner, Jeremy Smith, must receive thanks that can't fail to be woefully inadequate. I owe a debt to him for our endless conversations about money and politics, for his love, selfless support and patience as I wrestled with this text.

Notes

Introduction

1. Matthew Klein, 'Exorbitant Privileges, Burdens, etc. and the Implications for Fiscal Policy,' *The OverShoot*, 17 May 2025.
2. Gordon Brown, 'The "New World Order" of the Past 35 Years Is Being Demolished Before Our Eyes. This Is How We Must Proceed,' *Guardian*, 12 April 2025.
3. Geoffrey Ingham, *Money (What Is Political Economy?)*, Polity, 2020, p. 20.
4. Rachel Reeves, *The Everyday Economy*, 2018.
5. The American President Project, Franklin D. Roosevelt, Address at Madison Square Garden, New York City, 31 October 1936.
6. Karl Polanyi, *The Great Transformation*, Beacon Press 2001, p. 3.
7. Susan Strange, *Mad Money,* Manchester University Press, 1998, p. 3.
8. Lionel Barber, *Gambling Man: The Wild Ride of Japan's Masayoshi Son,* Penguin, 2024, p. 269.
9. Ibid., p. 270.
10. Ibid.
11. Ibid.

12. Lionel Barber, 'The Mystery of Masayoshi Son, SoftBank's Great Disruptor,' *Financial Times*, 21 September 2024.

13. Ibid.

14. Derek Saul, 'Japan's SoftBank Pledges $100 Billion – And 100,000 Jobs – To US For Trump's Second Term,' *Forbes*, 16 December 2024.

15. Matilda Hellman, Jenny Cisneros Ornberg and Charles Livingstone, 'Gambling Policy Studies: A Field That Is Growing in Size and Complexity', *Addiction Research and Theory*, 14 July 2017.

16. See Alexander Zevin, *Liberalism at Large: The World According to the Economist,* Verso, 2021.

17. Stanford Center on China's Economy and Institutions, 'The Rise of Wealth, Private Property, and Income Inequality in China,' 1 August 2023.

18. Matthew Klein and Michael Pettis, *Trade Wars Are Class Wars*, Yale University Press, 2020.

19. The World Bank, 'The Global Findex Database', 2021.

20. Erica Stanford, *Crypto Wars: Faked Deaths, Missing Billions and Industry Disruption*, Kogan Page, 2021.

21. Susan Strange, *Casino Capitalism,* Basil Blackwell, 1986.

22. Susan Strange, *Mad Money*, Manchester University Press, 1998, p. 3. Also, Nat Dyer, 'Susan Strange: A Great Thinker or a "Journalist"?', natdyer.com, 27 February 2019.

23. See the Financial Stability Board, *Global Monitoring Report on Non-Bank Financial Intermediation 2023*, 18 December 2023.

24. Claudio Borio, *On Money, Debt, Trust and Central Banking*, BIS, 2018, p. 1.

25. Quinn Slobodian, *Globalists: The End of Empire and the Birth of Neoliberalism*, Harvard University Press, 2018, p. 6.

26. Quinn Slobodian, *Crack-Up Capitalism: Market Radicals and the Dream of a World Without Democracy*, Allen Lane, 2023, p. 82.

27. Guy Standing, *The Blue Commons: Rescuing the Economy of the Sea*, Penguin Random House, 2022, p. 2.

28. I am grateful for discussions, support and the insights of this chapter to David Gee, formerly Senior Adviser to the European Environment Agency, Copenhagen, and Associate Fellow Institute of Environment, Health and Societies, Brunel University London.

29. Polanyi, *The Great Transformation*, p. 4.

30. See Deborah D. Avant, Martha Finnemore and Susan K. Sell, *Who Governs the Globe?*, Cambridge University Press, 2012.

31. Martijn Konings, *The Bailout State: Why Governments Rescue Banks, Not People*, Polity, 2025.

32. CBS News, 'Fed Chair Jerome Powell's *60 Minutes* Interview on Economic Recovery from the Coronavirus Pandemic,' 17 May 2020.

33. Susan Strange, *The Retreat of the State: The Diffusion of Power in the World Economy*, Cambridge University Press, 1996, p. 111.

34. David Graeber, *The Ultimate, Hidden Truth of the World*, Farrar, Straus and Giroux, 2024.

1. The Origin of Today's 'Revolutionary Situation'

1. Quoted by Huw van Steenis, 'The "Nixon Shock" Might Help Us Make Sense of the Trump One. Events of 1971 Ushered in the Era of Modern Finance', *Financial Times*, 13 April 2025.

2. Huw van Steenis, 'The "Nixon Shock" Might Help Us Make Sense of the Trump One'. But also in Jeffreye E. Garten, *Three Days at Camp David: How a Secret Meeting in 1971 Transformed the Global Economy*, Harper, 2021, p. 77.

3. See Garten, *Three Days at Camp David*.

4. Eric Helleiner, *Forgotten Foundations of Bretton Woods: International Development and the Making of the Postwar Order*, Cornell University Press, 2014.

5. Lord John Maynard Keynes, House of Lords, 18 May 1943, Vol 127, pp. 521–64.

6. Robert Skidelsky, *Inventing the World's Money*, New York Review of Books, 9 January 2014. Review of Ben Steil's *The Battle of Bretton Woods; John Maynard Keynes, Harry Dexter White and the Making of a New World Order.*

7. Eric Helleiner, *States and the Reemergence of Global Finance: From Bretton Woods to the 1990s*, Cornell University Press, 1994, p. 33.

8. Van Steenis, 'The "Nixon Shock"'; Helleiner, *States and the Reemergence of Global Finance*, p. 49.

9. See Alex J. Pollock, 'Fifty Years Without Gold', R Street, 16 August 2021.

10. 'Money: De Gaulle v. the Dollar', *Time Magazine*, 12 February 1965.

11. Helleiner, *States and the Reemergence of Global Finance*, p. 102.

12. Barry Eichengreen makes no mention of the 'Nixon Shock' of 1971. He writes: 'over the weekend of August 13, the Nixon administration closed the gold window, suspending the commitment to provide gold to official foreign holders of dollars at $35 an ounce or any other price. Rather than consulting with the IMF, it communicated its program to the managing director of the Fund as a fait accompli' (*Globalizing Capital: A History of the International Monetary System*, Princeton University Press, 2008, p. 131).

13. Helleiner, *States and the Reemergence of Global Finance*, p. 108.

14. José Antonio Ocampo *Special Drawing Rights and the Reform of the Global Reserve System*, IPD, August 2010.

15. J. A. Hobson, *Imperialism: A Study of the History, Politics and Economics of the Colonial Powers in Europe and America*, Adansonia Press, 2018 (1902).

16. Van Steenis, 'The "Nixon Shock"'.

17. Ann Pettifor, ed., *The Real World Economic Outlook. The Legacy of Globalization: Debt and Deflation*, Palgrave Macmillan, 2003. Also, Ann Pettifor, 2006. *The Coming First World Debt Crisis*, New Economics Foundation, 2003, p. xxvi.

18. Pettifor, *The Real World Economic Outlook*, 2003, p. 10

19. Cited in Jane D'Arista, *All Fall Down: Debt Deregulation and Financial Crises,* Edward Elgar, 2018, p. 95.

20. Quoted in Ed Conway, *The Summit: The Biggest Battle of the Second World War – fought behind closed doors,* Little, Brown, 2014, p. 365.

21. Michael Pettis, *The Great Rebalancing: Trade, Conflict and the Perilous Road Ahead for the World Economy,* Princeton University Press, 2013, p. 4.

22. Richard Kozul-Wright and Kevin Gallagher, 'Restoring Multilateralism, Phenomenal World website, 19 April 2025.

23. United States Census Bureau, *US International Trade in Goods and Services 1992 – Present,* census.gov.

24. See Martin Scheffel, Tom Krebs, VOXeu, CEPR, *German Labour Reforms: Unpopular Success,* 20 September 2013.

25. Geoff Tily, *From the Doom Loop to an Economy for Work, not Wealth,* TUC, February 2023.

26. Ibid., p. 17.

27. Susan Strange, 'Globaloney? (Review Essay)', *Review of International Political Economy* 5 (4), 1998, 704–11.

28. Karl Polanyi, *The Great Transformation,* 1944, p. 3.

29. A. Claire Cutler, *Susan Strange and the Future of Global Political Economy,* RIPE Series in Global Political Economy, p. 140.

30. Quoted in Michael Pettis and Matthew Klein, *Trade Wars are Class Wars,* 2020, p. 6.

31. Ibid, p. 7.

32. Hobson, *Imperialism.* Pettis and Klein, *Trade Wars Are Class Wars,* p. 58.

33. Hobson, *Imperialism,* p. 60.

34. Wolfgang Streeck, *Taking Back Control? States and State Systems After Globalism,* Verso, 2024, p. 41.

35. Ibid.

36. William J. Ripple et al. 'World Scientists' Warning of Climate Emergency', *BioScience* 71(9), September 2021, pp. 894–8.

37. Emily Sohn, *Climate Change and the Rise and Fall of Civilizations*, NASA, Global Climate Change, 20 January 2014.

2. Money and Power

1. See Ann Pettifor, *The Coming First World Debt Crisis*, Palgrave Macmillan, 2006, pp. 34–43.
2. See Mathias Schmelzer, *Freedom for Capital: The Mont Pèlerin Society and the Origins of the Neoliberal Monetary Order,* Verso, 2025, p. ix.
3. Costas Mourselas, 'Hedge Fund Elliott Warns White House Is Inflating Crypto Bubble that "Could Wreak Havoc"', *Financial Times*, 30 January 2025.
4. Ibid.
5. Ibid.
6. See Dan Alexander, 'Trump's Crypto Assets Are Nonsense. The Cash They Throw Off Is Very Real', forbes.com, 22 January 2025.
7. The White House, 23 January 2025, Presidential Actions. Executive Order. *Strengthening American Leadership in Digital Financial Technology.*
8. Trevor Jackson, 'The Ungovernable Economy', *New York Review of Books*, 25 January 2025.
9. Karl Polanyi, *The Great Transformation: The Political and Economic Origins of Our Time,* Beacon Press, 2001, p. 3.
10. The data on wealth inequality sourced from: Laurie Macfarlane, 'How Trump 2.0 Could Herald a New Age of Authoritarian Capitalism', opendemocracy.net, 20 January 2025.
11. See Daron Acemoglu, 'The Real Threat to American Prosperity', *Financial Times*, 8 February 2025.
12. Stefan Eich, 'Old Utopias, New Tax Havens: the Politics of Bitcoin in Historical Perspective', in Phillip Hacker (ed.), *Regulating Blockchain: Techno-Social and Legal Challenges*, Oxford, 2019.

13. John Maynard Keynes, *Essays in Persuasion*, 1931, p. 126. *The Speeches of the Bank Chairmen* (1924–1927).

14. See Karl Polanyi, *The Bennington Lectures,* 1940, first delivered at Bennington College, Vermont, and published by Policy Research in Macroeconomics (PRIME).

15. J. A. Hobson, *Imperialism. The Study of the History, Politics and Economics of the Colonial Powers in Europe and America*, Adansonia Press, 2018 (1902).

16. Matthew Klein and Michael Pettis, *Trade Wars Are Class Wars*, Yale University Press, 2020, p. 1.

17. Karl Polanyi, *The Bennington Lectures. Lecture 1. The Passing of 19th Century Civilization,* Policy Research in Macroeconomics (PRIME), primeeconomics.org, p. 13.

18. Unpublished and shared with the author in December 2024: Geoff Tily, *'Betrayal' Reconsidered: The General Theory, (Distributional) Macroeconomics and (Macrodynamic) Econometrics.*

19. Ibid.

20. E. Napoletano, 'What Is DeFi? Understanding Decentralized Finance', forbes.com, 28 April 2023.

21. Stefan Eich, 'Old Utopias, New Tax Havens: the Politics of Bitcoin in Historical Perspective', in Phillip Hacker (ed.), *Regulating Blockchain: Techno-Social and Legal Challenges*, Oxford, 2019.

22. Ibid.

23. Friedrich Hayek, *Denationalisation of Money,* Institute of Economic Affairs, 1976.

24. John Law, *Money and Trade Considered with a Proposal for Supplying the Nation with Money,* Yale Law School, Lilian Goldman Law Library, 1705.

25. Hayek, *Denationalisation of Money*, p. 95.

26. John Maynard Keynes, *The General Theory of Employment, Interest and Money*, Harper Business, 1935, p. 353.

27. Nicholas Shaxson, *Treasure Islands: Tax Havens and the Men Who Stole the World*, Vintage Books, 2011, p. 8.

28. Alex Cobham, Miroslav Palansky, *State of Tax Justice 2024: Methodology Note on Estimating the Scale of Undeclared Offshore Wealth and Related Tax Revenue losses,* Tax Justice Network, November 2024.

29. Ibid.

30. Susan Strange, 'What Theory? The Theory in Mad Money', CSGR Working Paper No. 18/98, Centre for the Study of Globalisation and Regionalisation, December 1998.

31. Ibid.

32. Ibid.

33. Paul McCulley, 'Comments Before the Money Marketeers Club: "Playing Solitaire with a Deck of 51, with Number 52 on Offer"', Pimco.com, Global Central Bank Focus, April 2009.

34. John Levin and Antoine Malfroy-Camine, *Bank Lending to Private Equity and Private Credit Funds: Insights from Regulatory Data,* Federal Reserve Bank of Boston, 2 February 2025.

35. 'Global Monitoring Report on Non-Bank Financial Intermediation 2024', Financial Stability Board, 16 December 2024.

36. See Daniela Gabor and Jakob Vestergaard, 'Towards a Theory of Shadow Money', Institute for New Economics, April 2016.

37. Committee for a Responsible Federal Budget, 'Covid Response, Federal Reserve', covidmoneytracker.org, 21 October 2021.

38. Eric Milstein and David Wessel, 'What Did the Fed Do in Response to the COVID-19 Crisis?' Brookings Institute, 2 January 2024.

39. Max Matza, 'Jeff Bezos and the Secretive World of Superyachts', bbc.co.uk, 14 May 2021.

40. Jack Pitcher, 'Jeff Bezos Just Added a Record $13 Billion to His Fortune in a Single Day', time.com, 20 July 2020.

41. Matza, 'Jess Bezos and the Secretive World of Superyachts'.

42. Alex Kasomitros, 'The Dangerous Growth of Shadow Banking', World Finance.com, 17 January 2023.

43. P. Lysandrou and A. Nesvetailova, 'The Role of Shadow Banking Entities in the Financial Crisis: a Disaggregated View', *Review of International Political Economy* 22(2), 2014, pp. 257–79.

44. Lisa Adkins, Melinda Cooper and Martijn Konings, *The Asset Economy*, Polity, 2020, p. 16.

45. BNP Paribas press release, 'BNP Paribas Investment Partners temporarily suspends the calculation of the Net Asset Value of the following funds: Parvest Dynamic ABS, BNP Paribas ABS EURIBOR and BNP Paribas ABS EONIA' , 9 August 2007, as archived by the St Louis Federal Reserve Bank.

46. See Andrew Duehren et al., 'Elon Musk's Team Now Has Access to Treasury's Payments System', *New York Times*, 1 February 2025.

47. Polanyi, *The Great Transformation*, p. 71.

48. Ibid., pp. 79–80.

49. Ibid., pp. 3–4.

3. Your Pension and the Asset Economy

1. See P. W. Ireland, 'Law and the Neoliberal Vision: Financial Property, Pension Privatization and the Ownership Society,' *Northern Ireland Legal Quarterly* 62(1), pp. 1–32.

2. Bank of England, 4 April 2014.

3. Boston Consulting Group, *20th Annual Global Asset Management Report,* 25 August 2022.

4. Ibid.

5. Ibid.

6. Speech by Andy Haldane, 'The Age of Asset Management?', Bank of England, 4 April 2014.

7. John Broadbent, Michael Palumbo and Elizabeth Woodman, *The Shift from Defined Benefit to Defined Contribution Pension Plans – Implications for Asset Allocation and Risk Management*, Bank for

International Settlements, December 2006. Srichander Ramaswamy, *The Sustainability of Pension Schemes*, BIS Working Papers No. 368, January 2012.

8. Guy Standing, 'The Precariat: Today's Transformative Class?' Great Transition Initiative, October 2018, greattransition.org.

9. Platform, *Offshore: Oil and Gas Workers' Views on Industry Conditions and the Energy Transition,* greenpeace.org.uk, October 2020.

10. Edwin Heathcote, 'How Thatcherism Laid the Foundations of the Housing Crisis: "Municipal Dreams" Explores what Happened when Decent Housing Came to Be Seen as an Unaffordable Luxury,' *Financial Times*, 1 June 2018.

11. Razak Musah Baba, 'KKR Expands UK Residential Portfolio with £100m Manchester Acquisition,' realassets.ipe.com, 15 April 2025.

12. Denise Garcia Ocampo and Carlos Lopez Moreira, 'Uncertain Waters: Can Parametric Insurance Help Bridge NatCat Protection Gaps?', BIS Financial Stability Institute, *FSI Insights* 62, p. 3.

13. 'Fed's Powell Says Some Areas of US May Be "Uninsurable" in Next Decade', *ABA Banking Journal*, 18 February 2025.

14. US Senate Finance Committee SD-215, 6 March 2025.

15. Lisa Adkins, Melinda Cooper, Martijn Konings, *The Asset Economy*, Polity Press, 2020, p. 36.

16. Ibid., p. 39; A. Darling, 'Speech by the Chancellor of the Exchequer, the Rt. Hon. Darling MP, to the CBI Annual Conference,' 27 November 2007.

17. See Stefano Corradin, Florian Heider and Marie Hoerov, 'On Collateral: Implications for Financial Stability and Monetary Policy,' ECB Working Paper Series.

18. Ann Pettifor, 'Asset Valuation as the Name of the Capitalist Game: How What Was Done to the *Spectator* Could Be Done to Your Investment, Pension', *System Change* substack, 19 September 2024.

19. Andrew Neil, 'Andrew Neil Jumps Ship', bellacaledonia.org.uk, 10 September 2024.

20. Simon M. Potter, 'Some Observations and Lessons from the Crisis', Third Annual Connecticut Bank and Trust Company Economic Outlook Breakfast, Hartford, Connecticut, 7 June 2010.

21. Press release, 'BNP Paribas Investment Partners Temporally Suspends the Calculation of the Net Asset Value of the Following Funds: Parvest Dynamic ABS, BNP Paribas ABS EURIBOR and BNP PARIBAS ABS EONIA', BNP Paribas, 9 August 2007.

22. Richard Partington, 'MPs Launch Inquiry into Pensions Crisis Sparked by Mini-Budget,' *Guardian*, 24 October 2022.

23. Kriti Mehrotra, 'Where Is Jan Marsalek Now? Has Wirecard's Ex-COO Been Found?', *The Cinemaholic*, 16 September 2022.

24. Paul Murphy, 'The Fund Managers That Kept Faith with Wirecard', *Financial Times*, 19 June 2020.

25. Daniela Gabor, Yannis Dafermos, Jo Michell, 'Minsky Was a Shadow Banker,' *Rebuilding Macroeconomics*, 22 January 2019.

26. Joscha Wullweber, *Central Bank Capitalism: Monetary Policy in Times of Crisis*, Stanford University Press, 2024, p. 101.

27. Ibid., p. 105.

28. Daniela Gabor, 'Revolution Without Revolutionaries: Interrogating the Return of Monetary Financing', Transformative Responses, Heinrich Böll Foundation, 2021.

29. Rajdeep Sengupta and Fei Xue, 'The Global Pandemic and Run on Shadow Banks', Federal Reserve Bank of Kansas City, 11 May 2020.

30. 'Global Monitoring Report on Non-Bank Financial Intermediation 2023', Financial Stability Board (FSB), 18 December 2023.

31. Robin Wigglesworth, 'Where Will Private Equity Aim Its $9 Trillion Money Hose?', *Financial Times*, 18 July 2024.

32. For a study of the corruption and fraud characteristic of the world's art markets, see Orlando Whitfield's *All That Glitters: A Story of Friendship, Fraud and Fine Art,* Profile Books, 2024.

4. Speculation and Our Daily Bread

1. Mark Hallett and Christine Riding, *Hogarth: The South Sea Scheme c. 1721*, Tate Publishing, 2007, p. 57.
2. Ibid.
3. Cited in Lynn A. Stout, 'Irrational Expectations', *Legal Theory* 3, 227, 1997.
4. Ibid.
5. Ibid., p. 229.
6. Axel Wion Monica Pesce, Armando Luciano and Sofia Noelle Gonzalex, *The Role of Commodity Traders in Shaping Agricultural Markets. Oligopoly and Vertical Integration: ABCDs Emerging Players, Novel Strategies, and Potential EU Intervention*, Directorate General for Internal Polices, European Parliament, Policy Department, Structural and Cohesion Policies: Research for Agri Committee, March 2024, p. 3.
7. Ibid.
8. Myriam Vander Stichele, 'How Financialisation Influences the Dynamics in the Food Supply Change', SOMO Centre for Research on Multilateral Organisations, September 2014.
9. Tejvan Pettinger, 'Explaining Supply and Demand', economicshelp. org, 25 February 2020.
10. Ibid.
11. Anuradha Mittal, 'The 2008 Food Price Crisis: Rethinking Food Security Policies', UN Trade and Development (UNCTAD), June 2009.
12. Ibid., p. 5.
13. 'The State of Food Insecurity in the World', Food and Agriculture Organization of the United Nations, 2009.
14. 'Commodity Market Speculation: The Risk to Food Security and Agriculture', US Institute for Agriculture and Trade Policy, 2008, p. 4.

15. Ben Rooney, 'Senate Takes on Oil, Food Speculators', cnnmoney. com, 20 May 2008.

16. Brett Christophers, *The Price Is Wrong: Why Capitalism Won't Save the Planet,* Verso, 2024.

17. Martin Wolf, 'What We Must Still Learn About the Great Inflation Disaster', *Financial Times,* 29 April 2024.

18. 'Global Cost-of-Living Crisis Catalyzed by War in Ukraine Sending Tens of Millions into Poverty,' United Nations Development Programme (UNDP), 7 July 2022.

19. 'Food for Thought. The Role of Food Prices in the Cost-of-Living Crisis', Resolution Foundation, 19 May 2023.

20. Megan Blake, *The Rise of Food Insecurity in England: Using Food Ladders to Overcome the Barriers,* University of Sheffield, May 2024.

21. Kabir Agarwal, Thin Lei Win and Margot Gibbs, '"Betting on Hunger": Market Speculation Is Contributing to Global Food Insecurity', *The Wire,* 6 May 2022.

22. Taylor Pearce, 'Orbán's Victory and the Politics of Economy', Official Monetary and Financial Institutions Forum, 7 April 2022.

23. Gavin Mortimer, 'Marine Le Pen Is Revelling in the Mayhem of Macron', *Spectator,* 2 May 2023.

24. Lynn A. Stout, *The Legal Origin of the 2008 Credit Crisis,* UCLA School of Law, 25 February 2011.

25. US Department of the Treasury, *Report of the President's Working Group on Financial Markets: Over-the-Counter Derivatives Markets,* November 1999.

26. Lynn A. Stout, 'Bettting the Bank: How Derivatives Trading Under Conditions of Uncertainty Can Increase Risks and Erode Returns in Financial Markets', Cornell Law Faculty Publications 445, scholarship.law.cornell.edu, Fall 1995, emphasis added.

27. 'Hedge Fund Operations Risks. Brooksley Born Testimony,' C-Span, 2 October 1998.

28. In Germain Randall, ed., *Susan Strange and the Future of Global*

Political Economy (RIPE Series in Global Political Economy), Routledge, 2016, p. 135.

29. Ibid.

30. Ibid.

31. Axel Wion et al., *The Role of Commodity Traders in Shaping Agricultural Markets*, p. 36.

32. Lynn Stout, *Why Re-regulating Derivatives Can Prevent Another Disaster*, Harvard Law School Forum on Corporate Governance, 21 July 2009.

33. Lynn A. Stout, 'How Deregulating Derivatives Led to Disaster, and Why Re-Regulating Them Can Prevent Another,' Cornell Law School, 1 January 2009.

34. Lynn A. Stout, 'Why Re-regulating Derivatives Can Prevent Another Disaster', Harvard Law School Forum on Corporate Governance, 21 July 2009.

35. Axel Wion et al., *The Role of Commodity Traders in Shaping Agricultural Markets*, p. 11.

36. Isabella Weber et al., *Buffer Stocks Against Inflation: Public Food Stocks for Price Stabilisation and Their Contribution to the Transformation of Food Systems*, Heinrich Böll Foundation, June 2024.

37. Ibid., p. 18.

5. Playing Poker with the Energy System

1. 'Global Monitoring Report on Non-Bank Financial Intermediation 2023,' Financial Stability Board, 18 December 2023.

2. Carlotta Breman and Servaas Storm, 'Betting on Black Gold: Oil Speculation and US Inflation (2020–2022)', *International Journal of Political Economy* 52, 2, 2023, pp. 153–80.

3. Shetland Islands Council, *Energy Production and Usage*, shetland. gov.uk, 2024.

4. Ibid.

5. Cited by Brett Christophers, *The Price Is Wrong: Why Capitalism Won't Save the Planet,* Verso, 2024, p. 167.

6. Olly Bartrum, 'Electricity Market', Institute for Government, 15 September 2022.

7. 'For the First Time, UK Household Electricity Prices Rose to Levels Higher than Those in Any EU Country', Nesta, 20 June 2024.

8. Iona Stewart, 'Why Is Cheap Renewable Energy So Expensive on the Wholesale Market?', House of Commons, 14 September 2023.

9. Paul Bolton and Iona Stewart, 'Domestic Energy Prices', House of Commons Library, 8 July 2024.

10. Jorge Liboreiro, 'Energy Crisis: How a Dutch Market Sets Prices for Gas for the Whole of Europe', *Euronews*, 30 August 2022.

11. 'Trade and Invest with the World's Leading Online Trading Provider', IG.com.

12. Carol Davenport and Lisa Friedman, 'How One Senator Doomed the Democrats' Climate Plan', *New York Times*, 15 July 2022.

13. Breman and Storm, 'Betting on Black Gold', p. 154. Citing Eckaus, *The Oil Price Really Is a Speculative Bubble,* MIT Centre for Energy and Environmental Policy Research working Paper, MIT Sloan School of Management, 2008.

14. Breaking Market News, @financialjuice, Twitter/X, 17 June 2022.

15. Rupert Russell, *Price Wars: How Chaotic Markets Are Creating a Chaotic World*, Doubleday, 2022, p. 147.

16. Robert Rapier, 'If Oil Companies Control Prices, Why Do They Ever Lose Money?', *Forbes*, 25 April 2022.

6. The Financialisation of Housing

1. David Dayen et al., 'Tackling the Housing Crisis: a Symposium on How Housing Unaffordability Happened and what Can Be Done', *American Prospect*, 11 December 2024.

2. Josh Ryan-Collins, Toby Lloyd and Laurie Macfarlane, *Rethinking*

the Economics of Land and Housing, Zed Books, 2017, p. 110 (Kindle edition).

3. Josh Ryan-Collins, 'Banking Cultures, Land Valuation, and "Doom Loops" (or, Why You Can't Afford a House in the UK)', LSE Blogs, 20 February 2016.

4. Òscar Jordà, Moritz Schularick and A. M. Taylor, 'Macrofinancial History and the New Business Cycle Facts', *NBER Macroeconomics Annual 2016*, vol. 31, 2017, pp. 213–63. Alana Semuels, 'When Wall Street Is Your Landlord', *Atlantic*, 13 February 2019.

5. Semuels, 'When Wall Street Is Your Landlord'.

6. ACCE Institute, 'Financialization of Single-Family Rentals: The Rise of Wall Street's New Rental Empire', PBS SoCal, 4 October 2017.

7. Providence Adu et al., 'Understanding Accra's Housing Market: An Exploratory Study Using User-Generated Data', *African Geographical Review* 43: 3, 2023; 'Where's the Most Expensive Real Estate in Latin America?' Bric Group, 14 November 2023, bric-group.com.

8. 'Ghana's Real Estate Boom: 3 Reasons Why Rental Properties Are Your Ticket to Financial Success', Waylead.org, 16 February 2024.

9. 'Medellin Real Estate: Property Buyer's Guide for Foreigners', medellinguru.com, 20 January 2025.

10. Josh Ryan-Collins, Toby Lloyd and Laurie Macfarlane, *Rethinking the Economics of Land and Housing*, Zed Books, 2017.

11. Dubai's Palm Jumeirah is an artificial offshore island. According to *Britannica* the islets were made mostly from sand dredged from the floor of the Persian Gulf, but the side of the crescent that is exposed to the open sea was shored up with stones and boulders from the mainland. See Robert Lewis, 'Palm Jumeirah', britannica.com.

12. Martin Wolf, 'In Defence of Democratic Capitalism', *Financial Times*, 20 January 2023.

13. Financial Stability Board (FSB), *Global Monitoring Report on Non-Bank Financial Intermediation 2024*, December 2024, p. 3.

14. Dominic O'Connell, 'The Collapse of Northern Rock Ten Years On', bbc.co.uk, 12 September 2017.

15. *Global Monitoring Report on Non-Bank Financial Intermediation*, FSB, December 2024.

16. 'World Economic Outlook Database', IMF.org, October 2024.

17. Karl Polanyi, *The Great Transformation: The Political and Economic Origins of Our Time,* Beacon Press, 2001, p. 68.

18. Michael Purton, '4 Practical Solutions to the World's Housing Crisis', World Economic Forum, 10 June 2024.

19. Our World in Data, 'Homelessness Rate, 2023', ourworldindata.org.

20. *The 2024 Annual Homelessness Assessment Report to Congress,* US Department of Housing and Urban Development, December 2024.

21. Ehsan Soltani, 'Mapped: How Global Housing Prices have Changed since 2010', Visual Capitalist, 2 April, 2023.

22. 'Average UK house Prices: 1980–2050', goodmove.co.uk, 1 February 2021.

23. Valentina Romei and Sam Fleming, 'Concern Over Housing Costs Hits Record High Across Rich Nations', *Financial Times*, 3 September 2024.

24. Ibid.

25. Nick Bano, *Against Landlords: How to Solve the Housing Crisis,* Verso, 2025, p. 1.

26. Valentina Romei, 'England. House Prices "Affordable" Only for Richest 10% in 2022–23', *Financial Times*, 9 December 2024.

27. Ibid.

28. Nick Bano, *Against Landlords: How to Solve the Housing Crisis,* Verso, 2025, p. 9 (Kindle edition).

29. Ian Mulheirn, 'Why Building 300,000 Houses per Year Won't Solve the Housing Crisis – and What Will', LSE BPP, 28 August 2019.

30. Ian Mulheirn, 'Tackling the UK Housing Crisis: Is Supply the Answer? A Summary', Tony Blair Institute for Global Change, 21 August 2019.

31. Josh Ryan-Collins, *The Demand for Housing as an Investment: Drivers, Outcomes and Policy Interventions to Enhance Housing Affordability in the UK*, Institute for Innovation and Public Purpose, October 2024.

32. Ibid.

33. Nick Bano, *Against Landlords: How to Solve the Housing Crisis*, Verso, 2025, p. 32.

34. Ibid.

35. Ryan-Collins, *The Demand for Housing as an Investment*.

36. Marko Bardoscia et al., *The Impact of Prudential Regulations on the UK Housing Market and Economy: Insights from an Agent-Based Model*, Bank of England, Staff Working Paper no. 1,066, March 2024.

37. 'Speculation Tax on Property Sales in Germany', Berlinmaegleren, 15 May 2024.

38. Josh Ryan-Collins, *Why Can't You Afford a Home?*, Polity, 2019, p. 110.

39. Ibid., p. 98.

7. Climate and the Casino

1. Gillian Tett, 'Wall Street's New Mantra: Green Is Good. Bankers Once Saw Tackling Climate Change as a Niche Issue. Now It Is a Chance to Fuel Future Profits. Is It a Turning Point?', *Financial Times*, 29 January 2021.

2. Ibid.

3. Ross Kerber, 'BlackRock Quits Climate Group as Wall Street Lowers Environmental Profile', Reuters, 9 January 2025.

4. Liliana Doganova, 'Is the Future Worth It?', *The Break-Down*, 18 July 2024.

5. Ibid.

6. Ibid.

7. Ibid.

8. Nicholas Stern, *The Economics of Climate Change: The Stern Review*, Cambridge University Press, 2006.

9. See Ann Pettifor, 'Nordhaus, "RefuseNiks", "FrontierNiks" and "LimitNiks": The "Single Number" Theory that Helped Nix Climate Change', *System Change*, 28 August 2023.

10. William Nordhaus, 'Critical Assumptions in the Stern Review on Climate Change', *Science* 317: 5835, 13 July 2007.

11. Intergovernmental Panel on Climate Change (IPCC), 'Key Economic Sectors and Services', in *Climate Change 2014 – Impacts, Adaptation and Vulnerability. Part A Global and Sectoral Aspects: Working Group II Contribution to the IPCC Report*, Cambridge University Press, 2014, pp. 659–708 (emphasis added).

12. Steve Keen, 'The Appallingly Bad Neoclassical Economics of Climate Change', *Globalizations* 18, 2021.

13. Bob Berwyn, 'Extreme Climate Impacts from Collapse of a Key Atlantic Ocean Current Could be Worse Than Expected, a New Study Warns', *Inside Climate News*, 9 February 2024.

14. Ibid.

15. Urgewald, 'Too Much in Oil and Gas, Still Too Much in Coal', *Investing in Climate Chaos*, updated 2024.

16. Roxana Bardan, 'NASA Confirms 2024 Warmest Year on Record', nasa.gov, 10 January 2025.

17. Ibid.

18. 'The 2024 Global and Gas Exit List: More Loss and Damage Ahead', urgewald.org, 12 November 2024.

19. Ibid.

20. *Banking on Climate Chaos: Fossil Fuel Finance Report 2024*, Banking on Climate Chaos, 13 May 2024, p. 4.

21. See Brett Christophers, *The Price Is Wrong: Why Capitalism Won't Save the Planet*, Verso, 2024; Jonathan Ford, 'The Price Is Wrong – Brett Christophers on Saving the Planet', *Financial Times*, 22 February 2024.

22. Tara Laan et al., *Burning Billions: Record Public Money for Fossil Fuels Impeding Climate Action,* International Investment for Sustainable Development, 21 November 2023.

23. Financial Stability Board (FSB), *Global Monitoring Report on Non-Bank Financial Intermediation,* 16 December 2024.

24. Jeff Masters and Bob Henson, 'The Role of Climate Change in the Catastrophic 2025 Los Angeles Fires', Yale Climate Connections, 9 January 2025.

25. Laurence Darmiento and Summer Lin, 'First, They Lost Their Home Insurance. Then, L.A. Fires Consumed Their Homes', *Los Angeles Times*, 12 January 2025.

26. Dave Jones, 'We're Marching Steadily Toward an Uninsurable Future', Barrons.com, 20 July 2023.

27. IMF, Global Financial Stability Report, *Chapter Two, Non-Bank Financial Intermediaries: Vulnerabilities and Tighter Financial Conditions,* April 2023, p. 65.

28. Ibid.

29. Annalaura Ianiro, Christian Weistroffer and Sebastiano Michele Zema, 'Synthetic Leverage and Margining in Non-Bank Financial Institutions', ECB, May 2022.

30. IMF, 'Non-Bank Financial Intermediaries: Vulnerabilities and Tighter Financial Conditions', in *Global Financial Stability Report*, April 2023, p. 71.

31. Ibid.

32. Gary W. Yohe, 'I'm an Economist. Here's Why I'm Worried the California Insurance Crisis Could Trigger Broader Financial Instability', *The Conversation*, 21 January 2025.

33. *Planetary Solvency: Risks and Recommendations*, Institute and Faculty of Actuaries (IFoA), 16 January 2025.

34. Trevor Jackson, interviewed by Irza Waraich, 'The Ungovernable Economy', *New York Review of Books*, 25 January 2025.

8. The Need for System Change

1. Nat Dyer, *Ricardo's Dream: How Economists Forgot the Real World and Led Us Astray*, Bristol University Press, 2024, p. 90.

2. Colin Tudge, 'Colin Tudge's biography', Colin Tudge's Great Re-Think, updated 2024.

3. Colin Tudge, *The Great Re-Think: A 21st Century Renaissance,* Pari Publishing, 2021, p. 56.

4. Barry Eichengreen, 'Can the Dollar Remain King of Currencies?' *Financial Times*, 22 March 2025.

5. Colin Tudge, *The Great Re-Think.*

6. J. M. Keynes, 'National Self-Sufficiency', *Yale Review*, 1 July 1933.

7. J. A. Hobson, *Imperialism: A Study of the History, Politics and Economics of the Colonial Powers in Europe and America*, Adansonia Press, 2018 (1902), p. 41.

8. Mathew Lawrence, 'Power to the People: The Case for a Publicly Owned Generation Company', Common Wealth, 26 September 2022.

9. For more on such shocks see Viral V. Acharya, Nicola Cetorelli and Bruce Tuckman, 'The Growing Risk of Spillovers and Spillbacks in the Bank–NBFI Nexus', *Liberty Street Economics*, Federal Reserve Banks of New York, 20 June 2024.

10. Joscha Wullweber, *Central Bank Capitalism: Monetary Policy in Times of Crisis,* Stanford University Press, 2024, pp. xi–xii.

11. Jonathan Guthrie, 'Meltdown – The Greed that Destroyed Credit Suisse', *Financial Times*, 18 March 2025.

12. Geoff Tily, *Keynes Betrayed*, Palgrave Macmillan, 2007, p. 32.

13. J. M. Keynes, *The General Theory of Employment, Interest and Money*, pp. 375–6, in Volume VII of *The Collective Writings of John Maynard Keynes*, Royal Economic Society, 1973 (emphasis added).

14. Ibid., p. 376 (emphases added).

15. J. M. Keynes, 'National Self-sufficiency', Yale Review, 1 July 1933.

16. Keynes, *The General Theory*, p. 382,

17. Ibid., p. 382.

18. Keynes, 'National Self-sufficiency', 1 July 1933.

19. Ibid (emphasis added).

20. Ibid.

21. F. A. Hayek, *Denationalisation of Money*, Institute of Economic Affairs, 9 April 2008.

22. Oliver Bullough, *Moneyland: Why Thieves and Crooks Now Rule the World and How to Take It Back,* Profile Books, 2018, p. 29.

23. Stephen Miran, *A User's Guide to Restructuring the Global Trading System*, Hudson Bay Capital, November 2024.

24. *Implement a Market Access Charge: No Tax Cut Is Free*, Compass, 11 February 2025.

25. Ibid.

26. Matthew C. Klein and Michael Pettis, *Trade Wars Are Class Wars*, Yale University Press, 2020, p. 221.

27. Miran, *A User's Guide to Restructuring the Global Trading System*.

28. 'Survey Reveals Majority of Americans Still Living Paycheck to Paycheck', PR Newswire, 25 September 2024.

29. Rogé Karma, 'Buy, Borrow, Die. How to Be a Billionaire and Pay No Taxes', *Atlantic*, 17 March 2025.

30. Ibid.

31. Financial Stability Board, *Global Monitoring Report on Non-Bank Financial Intermediation*, fsb.org, 2024.

32. Joscha Wullweber, *Central Bank Capitalism: Monetary Policy in Times of Crisis,* Stanford University Press, 2024, p. 3.

33. Professor Massimo Amato of Bocconi University and Lucio Gobbi of Trento University, in an unpublished paper shared with the author.

34. Thomas Mann, *Buddenbrooks*, Vintage Classics, 2025, p. 494.

35. See Ed Conway, *The Summit: The Biggest Battle of the Second World War*, Little, Brown, 2014, p. 244.

36. Lord John Maynard Keynes, *Hansard*, Vol. 127, 18 May 1943, pp. 521–64.

37. Robert Skidelsky in his biography of Keynes (*John Maynard Keynes, 1883–1946: Economist, Philosopher, Statesman*, Penguin, 2004, p. 765) records that a 'little-noticed amendment allowed member countries to fix their currencies either to gold or to the dollar. This made the dollar, the only gold-convertible currency, the key currency of the new system.'

38. Conway, *The Summit*, p. 246.

39. Lord Keynes, House of Lords, *Hansard,* 'International Clearing Union', vol. 127, line 522, 18 May 1943.

40. Ibid.

41. Ibid.

42. Ann Pettifor, 'The Case for an African Payments Union: Lessons from the European Experience', Carnegie Endowment for International Peace, 19 December 2024.

43. Jane D'Arista, *All Fall Down: Debt, Deregulation and Financial Crises*, Edward Elgar Publishing, 2018.

44. Massimo Amato, Luca Fantacci and Lucio Gobbi, 'Regional Clearing Systems: from the European Payments Union to Current Initiatives Confronting Dollar Dominance', SSRN, 21 May 2024.

45. Quoted in Wolfgang Streeck, *Taking Back Control? States and State Systems After Globalism,* Verso, 2024, p. 289.

46. Phila Back, 'Living Like a Fungus', resilience.org, 13 March 2025.

Index

government assets 90–1
government debt, valuation 98
government intervention, speculation
    119–21
government spending 21
Graeber, David 29
grain markets
    food shock, 2005–8 111–12
    oligopolistic structure 106–7
    price setting and volatility 108–10
    speculation 106–8
    supply and demand 108–10
Great Depression 58, 166
Great Rethink, the 164–6
greenhouse gas emissions 30
Greenspan, Alan 115, 117, 184
Grenfell Tower fire 83
Grossman, Sanford 105
Guardian (newspaper) 93

Haldane, Andy 79
Hawley, Josh 176
Hayek, F. A. 22, 61–2, 66, 71, 174
hedge funds 19, 20–1, 67, 70, 91, 97,
    105, 111, 118–19, 133, 156, 157
hedging 104–5
Helleiner, Eric 34
Hobson, J. A. 12–13, 46–7, 57, 167
Hogarth, William 103–4
homelessness 139
housing and the housing market
    132–46
    affordability 132, 140, 143–6
    as financial investment 132
    financialised 142
    foreclosure crisis 133
    functions 134–5
    local conditions 135–6
    ownership 84
    prices 84, 132, 133–4, 137–40,
        142

as a privilege 134
    public sector privatisation 83–4
    rents 143, 144
    second homers 141
    speculation 141
    supply 140–3
Huang, Jensen 13
Hume, David 11
hyper-financialisation 91
hyperglobalisation 45, 179–80

imbalances, correcting 172–3
IMF 2, 35, 38, 56, 61, 78, 136–7,
    158–60, 183
imperialism 11–13, 46–8, 57
income inequality 40
India, food buffer stocks 120
inequality 2, 13–14, 44, 50
    acceleration of 73
    income 40
    obscene levels of 52
inflation 45, 55, 61, 105, 137–8,
    169–70
infrastructure
    necessity of appropriate 165
    ownership 167–8
injustice 50, 74
insecurity 22, 45
Institute for Economic Affairs 61
Institute of Actuaries 161
insurance industry 84–8, 104–5,
    158–62
interest rates 3, 5, 28, 29, 37, 63,
    168–72
Intergovernmental Panel on
    Climate Change (IPCC)
    150–1, 153
International Clearing Union
    (ICU) 33–4, 186–7
international economic order,
    governance 43–4